DEVELOPING LANGUAGE SKILLS
Reading 1

Introducing Prose, Plays, Poems

Sheila Freeman and Esther Munns

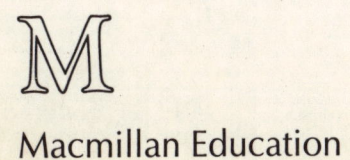

M

Macmillan Education

To our parents

© Sheila Freeman and Esther Munns 1987

All rights reserved. No reproduction, copy or transmission
of this publication may be made without written permission.

No paragraph of this publication may be reproduced, copied
or transmitted save with written permission or in accordance with the provisions
of the Copyright Act 1956 (as amended).

Any person who does any unauthorised act in relation to
this publication may be liable to criminal prosecution and civil claims for
damages.

First published 1987

Published by
MACMILLAN EDUCATION LTD
Houndmills, Basingstoke, Hampshire RG21 2XS
and London
Companies and representatives
throughout the world

Designed by Linda Reed

Printed in Hong Kong

British Library Cataloguing in Publication Data
Freeman, Sheila
Introducing prose, plays, poems
1. Readers — 1950–
I. Title   II. Munns, Esther
428.6   PE1121
ISBN 0–333–39801–7

Acknowledgements

The authors and publishers wish to thank the following who have kindly given permission for the use of copyright material:

Agriculture and Construction Press for recipe 'Harvest Rabbit' from *Farmhouse Fare*, Countrywise Books; Anvil Press Poetry Ltd for 'A Child Half-asleep' from *Kon in Springtime* by Tony Connor, and University of Georgia Press for the same poem from *New and Selected Poems* by Tony Connor © (1982) University of Georgia Press; *Books for Keeps* for extract from Betsy Byars' article in the July 1982 issue; Cambridge University Press for 'Workings of the Wind' by J. Berry and 'I Like to Stay Up' by G. Nichols from *I Like That Stuff*, ed. M. Styles (1984); Century Hutchinson Ltd for 'The Maid Who Chose a Husband' from *The Woman in the Moon* by J. Riordan (1984); Chatto and Windus Ltd for 'About Friends' from *Spitfire on the Northern Line* by Brian Jones (1975); Collins Educational for an extract from *A Game of Soldiers* by J. Needle (1985); Victor Gollancz Ltd for an extract from *Bridge to Terabithia* by Katherine Paterson (1982); *The Gravesend Reporter* for article 'It's the boot for "Flopears"' by Paul John; Faber & Faber Ltd for 'Take One Home for the Kiddies' from *The Whitsun Weddings* by Philip Larkin; Hamish Hamilton Ltd for 'The Best Day of My Easter Holidays' from *Black Faces, White Faces* by Jane Gardam; William Heinemann Ltd for extracts from *Going Back* (1977) and *The Driftway* (1972) by Penelope Lively; Heinemann Educational Books for extracts from *Johnny Salter* by Aidan Chambers (1966), and *The Play of the Silver Sword* © 1982 by Ian Serraillier and S. Henson, adapted from Ian Serraillier, *The Silver Sword*, Jonathan Cape © 1956 I. Serraillier; David Higham Associates on behalf of E. Storey for an extract from *The Solitary Landscape*, Gollancz (1975), on behalf of J. Paton Walsh for an extract from *A Parcel of Patterns*, Penguin (1983), on behalf of Charles Causley for an extract from *The Gift of a Lamb*, Robson Books (1978), on behalf of Norman Nicholson for 'Scafell Pike' from *Sea to the West*, Faber & Faber (1981) and on behalf of Eleanor Farjeon for 'It Was Long Ago' from *Silver Sand and Snow*, Michael Joseph; ILEA Centre for Language in Primary Schools for an extract from *Language Matters*, No. 3 (1983); Julia MacRae Books for an extract from *Janey* by Bernard Ashley (1985); John Johnson Ltd on behalf of the Estate of Henry Treece for extracts from *Dreamtime* by Henry Treece and the play adaption of *Dreamtime* by S. Freeman & E. Munns; The Marvell Press for 'Myxomatosis' from *The Less Deceived* by Philip Larkin; Oxford University Press for 'The Rabbit Man' from *The Oxford Book of Nursery Rhymes*, eds Iona & Peter Opie (1955) and extracts from *On the Edge* by Gillian Cross (1984); Penguin Books Ltd for 'Dog in the Quarry' from *Selected Poems* by Miroslav Holub, trans. I. Milner & G. Theiner © M. Holub (1967), trans. © Penguin Books (1967), 'William's Version' from *Nothing to be Afraid of* by Jan Mark © (1977) (1980), 'The Bossy Young Tree' from *Gargling with Jelly* by Brian Patten © (1985), an extract from the cover text from *A Parcel of Patterns* by J. Paton Walsh (1983), an extract plus illustration from *The Tale of Peter Rabbit* by Beatrix Potter © Frederick Warne & Co. (1902), an extract from *The Way to Sattin Shore* by Philippa Pearce © (1983) and an extract from *The Fate of Jeremy Visick* by David Wiseman © (1982); Margaret Ramsay Ltd on behalf of Ray Jenkins for extracts from *Five Green Bottles* and *Why a Play?*. All rights whatsoever in this play are strictly reserved and application for performances, etc. should be made before rehearsal to Margaret Ramsay Ltd, 14a Goodwin's Court, St. Martin's Lane, WC2. No performance may be given unless a licence has been obtained; Routledge & Kegan Paul PLC for 'Children' from 'The Elephant' by Slawomir Mrozek in *Rebels* eds Jones et al; Vernon Scannell for 'The Climb and the Dream' and 'November Story'; Martin Secker & Warburg Ltd for 'You'll See' from Collected Poems 1952–83 by Alan Brownjohn (1983) and 'A Windy Day' from *The Poetical Works of Andrew Young*; Myfanwy Thomas for 'Thaw' from *Collected Poems* by Edward Thomas, Faber & Faber; A.P. Watt Ltd on behalf of Lady Herbert for 'At the Theatre' by A.P. Herbert, Methuen, London Ltd; Wolfhound Press for an extract from *All Things Come of Age* by Liam O'Flaherty (1977).

Acknowledgements

The authors also wish to thank Janet Hartley-Trigg for not only typing but caring about their manuscript; Steve Leach for his contribution to *The Climb and the Dream*; Pat and Jake Robson for the extract from their log 'A Parcel of Patterns' and all their colleagues and students in the teaching and learning profession.

The author and publishers wish to acknowledge the following illustrations:

Pages 7 and 8: From *The Highwayman* by Alfred Noyes, illustrated by Charles Keeping. Text © Alfred Noyes 1913 renewed 1941, illustrations © Charles Keeping 1981. Published by Oxford University Press.
Pages 9 and 10: From *A Parcel of Patterns* by Jill Paton Walsh, illustrations by Steve Braund. Published by Puffin Books.
Page 74: From *If At First You Do Not See*, illustrated and written by Ruth Brown. A Beaver Book published by Arrow Books 1985
Pages 75, 76, 77, 78 and 79: From *Come Away from the Water, Shirley*, illustrated by John Burningham. Published by Jonathan Cape Ltd.
Pages 100, 112, 222, 236 and 243: Illustrations by Aneurin Edwards.
Pages 119 and 120: From *Clocks and More Clocks*, illustrated and written by Pat Hutchins, reproduced by permission of The Bodley Head, London.
Page 121: From *Where the Wild Things Are*, illustrated and written by Maurice Sendak, reproduced by permission of The Bodley Head, London.
Pages 122 and 123: From *Granpa*, illustrated and written by John Burningham, published by Jonathan Cape Ltd.
Pages 125 and 126: From *The Mark on the Beach* by J. Holmwood.
Pages 133, 134, and 135: From *I Remember* by Dorfy, published by Tree Press, Mid-Northumberland Arts Group.
Pages 162 and 163: From *It's Your Turn, Roger*, illustrated and written by Susanna Gretz, reproduced by permission of The Bodley Head, London.
Page 164: From *Twin Talk* by Peter C. Heaslip, reproduced by permission of Methuen Children's Books, 1985.
Page 238: From *All Things Come of Age*, illustrated by Liam O'Flaherty, published by Wolfhound Press, 1977.
Page 239: Bodleian Library, Oxford. Engraving in the John Johnson Collection.
Page 242: From *The Tale of Peter Rabbit* by Beatrix Potter, © Frederick Warne & Co., 1902.
Page 247: Reece Winstone.

The publishers have made every effort to trace the copyright holders, but where they have failed to do so they will be pleased to make the necessary arrangements at the first opportunity.

Contents

Preface		3
1 Picking up clues		5
PICTORIAL	Pictures tell a story	5
NOVEL	*A Parcel of Patterns*, Jill Paton Walsh	9
DRAMA	*The Silver Sword*, Stuart Henson	18
VERSE	Picking up clues in poetry *Scafell Pike*, Norman Nicholson	26
2 Finding your voice and finding a focus		34
STORYTELLING	*I Like to Stay Up*, Grace Nichols	34
	A Story for Every Item, Harold Rosen	35
	Story by a first-year pupil	36
THE WRITER'S VOICE	*A Letter from Bhavana*	38
	I Can't Write No Pretty Poem, Toni Cade	42
	Bridge to Terabithia, Katherine Paterson	44
	How I Started Writing for Children, Gillian Cross and Betsy Byars	48
	Working with Children, Bernard Ashley	51
DRAMA	*Johnny Salter*, Aidan Chambers	53
FINDING A FOCUS	*A Dead Pig and My Father*, Nina Bawden	65
	Going Back, Penelope Lively	66
	Wind, Edward Storey	69
	Workings of the Wind, James Berry	70
	A Windy Day, Andrew Young	71
3 Shifting viewpoints		74
PICTURE BOOKS	*If At First You Do Not See*, Ruth Brown	74
	Come Away from the Water, Shirley, John Burningham	75
CHARACTERS IN FICTION	*The Best Day of My Easter Holidays*, Jane Gardam	80
	On the Edge, Gillian Cross	87
DRAMA	*A Game of Soldiers*, Jan Needle	101
VERSE	*Thaw*, Edward Thomas	112
	The Climb and the Dream, Vernon Scannell	113
	Take One Home for the Kiddies, Philip Larkin	117

Contents

4	Time passes	118

PICTURE BOOKS	*Clocks and More Clocks*, Pat Hutchins	119
	Where the Wild Things Are, Maurice Sendak	120
	Granpa, John Burningham	121
	The Mark on the Beach, Jo-Anne Holmwood and Elizabeth Cross	124
TIME IN VERSE	*You'll See*, Alan Brownjohn	128
	About Friends, Brian Jones	130
	It was Long Ago, Eleanor Farjeon	130
TIME PAST	*I Remember*, Dorfy	133
	The Way to Sattin Shore, Philippa Pearce	136
	The Fate of Jeremy Visick, David Wiseman	142
	The Driftway, Penelope Lively	145

5	Focus on dialogue	161

PICTURE BOOKS	*It's Your Turn, Roger*, Susanna Gretz	161
	Twin Talk, Peter C. Heaslip	164
SHORT STORY	*William's Version*, Jan Mark	165
NOVEL	*Janey*, Bernard Ashley	172
VERSE	*November Story*, Vernon Scannell	183
	The Bossy Young Tree, Brian Patten	184
DRAMA	*Five Green Bottles* – a play for radio, Ray Jenkins	188

6	Experimenting with form	201

VERSE	*A Dog in the Quarry*, Miroslav Holub (trans. George Theiner)	201
SHORT STORY	*Children*, Slawomir Mrozek	205
NOVEL INTO PLAY	*The Dream Time*, Henry Treece	212
VERSE PLAYS	*The Gift of a Lamb*, Charles Causley	223
PROSE INTO PLAY	*The Maid Who Chose a Husband*, retold by Efua Sutherland	229

7	Fact, feeling and form	235

ANTHOLOGY	*Tell Me About the Rabbits*	235
	The Private Life of the Rabbit, Lockley	235
	All Things Come of Age, Liam O'Flaherty	237
	Bye Baby Bunting	239
	Here I Am with My Rabbits	239
	Fifteen Rabbits, Felix Salten	240
	Harvest Rabbit, a recipe	241
	Peter Rabbit, Beatrix Potter	242
	The Private Life of the Rabbit, Lockley	242
	Myxomatosis, Philip Larkin	243
	Adolf, D.H. Lawrence	244
	'It's the Boot for Flopears'	246

Preface

From the authors: to teachers and their pupils

This book was written to help pupils to develop as active and more confident readers.

The selection and organisation of the literature has taken into account the fact that within the age and interest range for which we are writing there will be those pupils who are reluctant to read at all; some who experience difficulty in sustaining interest in reading; those who resist the challenge of a demanding author and yet others, already avid readers, who constantly need the stimulus of new material.

Our chapter headings suggest some of the skills that, as readers, we all need to acquire and go on developing. Readers need to be encouraged to:

- pick up the clues offered by the author, illustrator, publisher and reviewer in order to have immediate access to a new book;
- share all previous understanding of how stories work as well as their own experiences of living in the world;
- be aware of the different 'voices' in a story, poem or play;
- understand the writer's purpose in focusing on a particular incident or character;
- see people and events from more than one point of view;
- accept that literature can move us backwards and forwards in time and space while we remain seated in the present; and
- appreciate the particular form in which the writing is expressed and any differences it makes to the way in which we 'read' the story, poem or play.

Within each chapter, pupils are introduced to a wide range of literature. We have given careful thought to the order in which it appears but this does not preclude a teacher from selecting, from any chapter, those parts which support work already in progress.

We hope that our choice of longer extracts from new publications will encourage pupils to want to talk about and read whole books. What is equally important is that the suggestions for talk, writing and drama can be applied to any literature being read by individuals, groups, or the whole class.

A collection of recent paperback books, including a wide selection of picture books, would greatly support and further develop the aims of this book. It is acknowledged that picture books make pleasurable links for secondary pupils with previous reading experiences in their primary schools. In any case it is important that, as present sisters, brothers and babysitters and possibly future parents, teachers and librarians, all pupils should be kept up to date with the extensive range of quality picture books available. On a deeper level, by close examination of picture book stories and illustrations, we are helped towards a closer understanding of the creative process at work in both writers and readers.

Finally, since all language skills are closely related, our chief concern throughout this book is to suggest ways of working which we believe will result in pupils becoming independent thinkers, speakers, listeners, writers and readers.

1 Picking up clues

PICTORIAL
Pictures tell a story

From the very beginning of our lives, we are surrounded by print of all kinds. If you kept a log of all the written information that you observed in one day, the range would be enormous. Think about newspapers, letters, forms, signs, instructions, advertisement hoardings, sweet wrappings, rules for games and so on.

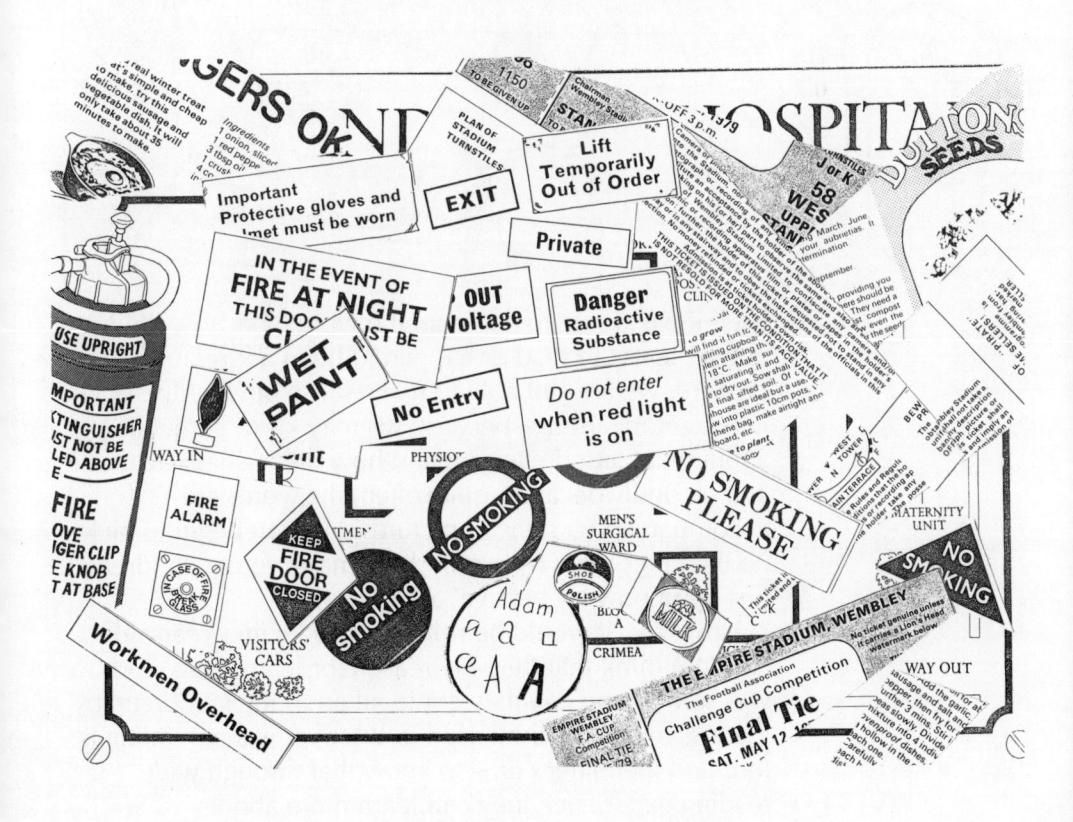

Picking up clues

Sometimes within one place, such as a laundrette, we are bombarded with information.

Even if we are unable to read the words, because we have not yet learnt to read or happen to be in a foreign country, we are still able to make sense of what the messages mean: first because we may know something about what laundrettes are and how they usually work, and secondly because, quite often, the words are accompanied by signs or pictures. We can begin to pick up the clues. This is, in fact, how many young children first learn how to 'behave' as readers.

However, it would be ridiculous to let five-year-old children think that the only reason for learning to read was so that one day they could all go to the laundrette by themselves! What they need to discover is that reading is fun, and then later come to know that through wide reading experience they can learn more about themselves, their real and imagined worlds.

Many of your first reading experiences will have been with wordless picture books, such as *The Snowman* by

PICTORIAL: Pictures tell a story

Raymond Briggs. Every child 'reads' a different story into this book. This is true of all books, even those in which the words on the page are the same for all of us, because, as readers, we each bring something of ourselves to a story during the reading of it.

Reading and talking

Think about all the reading you have been asked to do in this chapter so far – including the pictures.
- Talk about what you have read.
- Talk about how you read it. Did you have to re-read any part? Were you helped by reading anything out loud? Did you hold up your reading by stopping to talk about it?

Concentrate on these two illustrations by Charles Keeping.

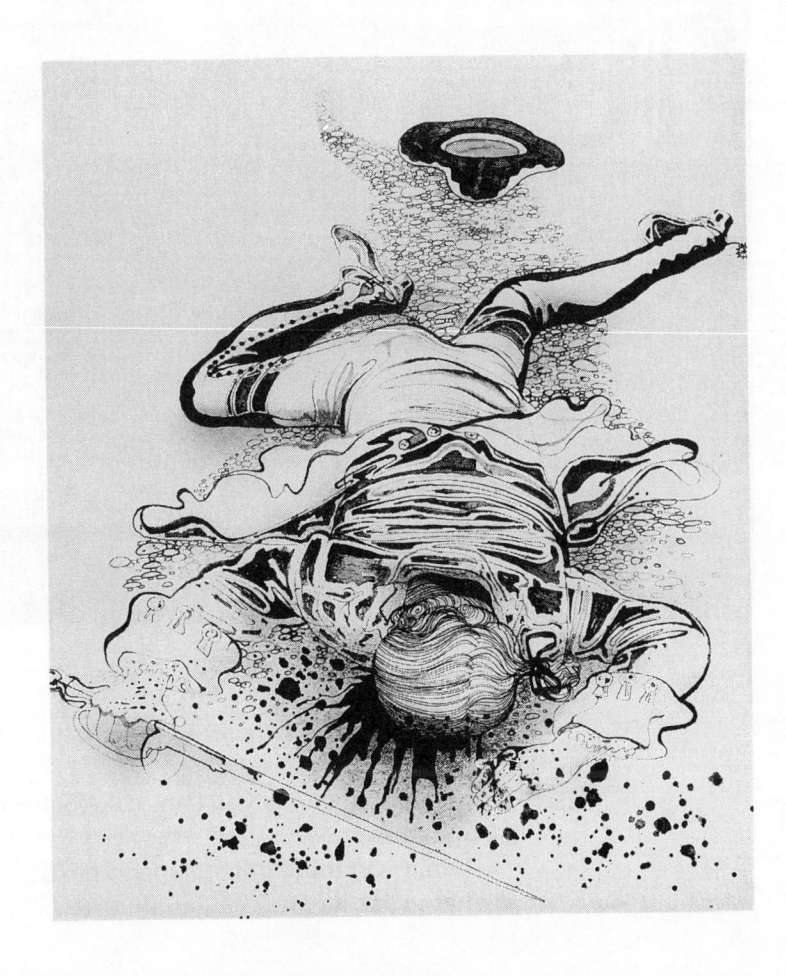

7

Picking up clues

- Talk about:
  - what you think might have happened in the story so far;
  - any connections you can make between the two pictures;
  - what you think might happen next.
- Share your ideas.

NOVEL

A Parcel of Patterns, Jill Paton Walsh

To become confident readers means that we must be prepared to make the most of all the clues that are given and sometimes to share the reading of a book with others, especially when we are engaged in reading a story as challenging as *A Parcel of Patterns* by Jill Paton Walsh.

First of all, look at the cover clues and the 'blurb description' that follow.

Picking up clues

> Puffin Plus
> ## A PARCEL OF PATTERNS
>
> The plague comes to the village of Eyam, possibly brought by a parcel of dress patterns from London. A young girl called Mall tells the story that begins on that fateful day.
>
> It is a story of the courage of individuals as the fearful disease progresses through the village, and it is also a tale of collective heroism, as the villagers make a vow to contain the plague within their own boundaries. The villagers' self-sacrifice forces Mall to make her own heartbreaking decision. She must not go to meet her beloved Thomas on the hills for fear of passing the sickness on to him – but how can she bear not to see him or at least to tell him how she is?
>
> *A Parcel of Patterns* is a powerful drama and a moving love story. Eyam (pronounced Eem) is a real village in Derbyshire, and many of the events in this evocative novel are based on what actually happened there in the year of the plague. The characters – the two rival parsons, the lovers Emmot and Roland, the brutal Marshall Howe whose strength is needed to bury so many dead, and Mall and Thomas themselves, as well as a host of villagers – come to life from the first page, and will stay with the reader long after the last page has been turned. This stunningly written novel is Jill Paton Walsh's finest and most compelling work to date.
>
> 'An outstanding piece of writing' – Naomi Lewis, The *Listener*
> 'An extraordinary and compelling *tour de force*' – Neil Philip, *The Times Educational Supplement*

Talking and writing

- Work in groups. Study in detail and talk about all the information given. Choose one person to take notes of the discussion. Remember to use all the clues provided as you predict what the story may be about.
- Make a list of questions which you expect your reading of the book to answer.
- Prepare your comments for a general class discussion.

When we begin to read a book, the author expects his or her readers to draw on previous experiences, knowledge and feelings which might help to make the story more real.

As a whole class, gather together and talk about any

NOVEL: *A Parcel of Patterns*, Jill Paton Walsh

background knowledge you already have to do with the plague and its effect on the village of Eyam.

One helpful way of reading a difficult novel is to keep a log-book in which you write:
- your first impressions;
- comments about characters;
- about the plot;
- about the style;
- anything you don't understand;
- questions you would like to ask;
- guesses about what might happen next;
- changes in your views about the story and the characters.

If two people or more are reading the same book, it is a good idea to exchange notes at certain agreed points in the story.

Here is an extract from a log kept by a mother and her thirteen-year-old son, Jake, during their shared reading of *A Parcel of Patterns*.

Doubtless you will be in the same position as we were when we began our reading; that is, we knew the outline of the plot, the villagers of Eyam decide to contain the plague within their own boundaries, and of the sacrifice this caused them. Beyond this we knew little, only the historical time and place; so we were ready to see not <u>what</u> would happen, but rather <u>how</u> it would happen.

What kinds of characters would there be? What would it feel like to be imprisoned by choice, and face death daily? How would the villagers come to their decision and who would instigate it?

Picking up clues

> These were the thoughts in our minds as we opened the book and read the first sentence:
>
> 'A parcel of patterns brought the Plague to Eyam.'
>
> Jake thought the beginning of the story had been a bit boring, as there had not been much speaking; later he felt it became more like a play. He also found it disconcerting not to know who the main character, who was speaking to us, was until page fourteen.
>
> This was something I had not noticed. Had I just assumed the character was a girl? The book is written in the first person:
>
> 'I see now that this task of writing I have undertaken I lack wit and skill and set things down awry.'
>
> When we searched back through the text I could see Jake was right; this main character, who is relating the story of Eyam is not revealed as a girl until page fourteen, and it isn't until page eighteen that we learn her name and age. We then discussed the reasons for the author withholding the information and wondered if it could be that she did not want the book to be seen as specifically a boys' or girls' book.
>
> As we noticed later the cover of the book is a 'give away' as there is a picture of a girl as the

main subject of the illustration. Actually we thought this a shame as it could suggest to boys that this book was not for them.

It is interesting that Jake used the word 'disconcerting' to describe his feelings when he did not know the sex of the main character. Does this mean he thinks it makes a difference whether this character is a boy or a girl? The phrase he used was 'Mal is just a person, we don't know any more'. I think that he is talking here about the difference between 'just a person' and 'a particular person'. And to be a 'particular person' we need to know more details.

By page thirty-three we had been introduced to many characters, and as with all books about groups of people it took quite a lot of effort to remember who was who. The period of the story is the Restoration, and we had some discussion about what this must have meant to a village which had Puritan values.

There are two parsons in the village, the old parson, Parson Stanley a Puritan, and the new parson Parson Momphesson. Parson Stanley refused to conform to the new ways and so he is replaced, although he remains in the village. We saw that this provided an interesting element as the two parsons confront each other.

Picking up clues

We take up the story at the point at which the new Parson, Momphesson, tells the villagers that, in order to stop the plague spreading to other places, no-one must leave the village.

As I have writ, we had been in a strange dullness that month of June, a liking not to know, a fearful quietness upon us; and that was broken all apart on the Sunday when Parson Momphesson told us he would close the churchyard. This he said to us in church after the end of the service, and at first we heard him, shivering in dismay, but quietly.

'My friends,' he said, 'such digging of graves, and digging again hard by, and filling of Plague corpses into pits under our very feet as we come to church, and, further, the bringing of bodies through the streets, past our doors, with putrefaction already working upon them, to reach the churchyard, all this seems now to hazard the living, which neither Our Lord God, nor those who are dead, would desire us to do. From today forward, therefore, shall there be none buried in the churchyard; but in the gardens, and upon the open hillside, wherever quickest it may be done, shall we consign them to the earth, and our prayers while yet the graves are open shall be but brief . . .'

'What? Not to lie in holy ground?' cried out a woman from the back of the church, I know not who.

John Stanley, the old parson's son, made answer at once, with, 'Fie! We are as near to heaven lying beneath our own thresholds as in any ground upon earth, be it or be it not priest-blessed!'

'We shall be scattered hither and yon, and how shall he find us at the Judgement Day?' wailed Joaney Hodge.

'Tush, tush!' said Agnes Sheldon. 'Think you it could be beyond the wit of God to find thee, should he wish? But more like when he gathers the just to his bosom, he will not be seeking thee!'

'Parson,' said quiet Robert Wood, 'can we not lay each man or woman a little further away from the next, but still within the churchyard?'

'My friend,' said Parson Momphesson, 'the churchyard

NOVEL: *A Parcel of Patterns*, Jill Paton Walsh

is but a small space; and there have been laid into it already some eighty-five of thy neighbours, in this black season . . .'

It was naming the number that did it, I think. But the words were no sooner spoken than a great cry went up, in every quarter of the church, some crying, 'We are dead! All dead!' and others, 'Flee neighbours! For our lives, neighbours, flee!'

'We must forsake Eyam utterly!' cried someone in a great voice. And folk began to rush forth from the church and pour out into the churchyard, taking to their heels as though they would run away in that very instant.

Parson Momphesson went through the vestry door, and ran like the wind, so that he reached the lych-gate before any, and hollered so loud and so fiercely, crying, 'Hear me! First hear me!' like a madman, that he stemmed the rush. The folk of Eyam were penned in the churchyard like sheep in a fold, and stood like sheep flinching from the dog, swaying and on tiptoe, trembling, all together braced, as though they would run off any moment, but none would go first, and so they were held, waiting for the Judas sheep to break away, which all would follow . . . and while they hesitated, Momphesson spoke.

'My friends, the safety of all the country round about is in our keeping. If you all flee away you will take the Plague with you, far and wide. You cannot escape death by flight; many of us are already infected, though we know it not . . .' At this a groan came from the crowd, and I in the midst of the press stood so close against my neighbour I knew not if I too had groaned or no. '. . . The invisible seeds of death are hidden within your clothing, and in the bundles you would carry with you, and in your very bodies; while not saving yourselves you will bring death upon countless others as you go. Oh, will you go to God and his judgement with the guilt for deaths innumerable and suffering untold upon your souls?'

As he said this the crowd broke; Lydia Kemp took up her skirt hem in her hand and ran away, going towards the corner of the churchyard furthest from where Momphesson barred the way, with others running after her, to climb over the low wall into the street. And so, I think, the flight would have taken place, had not she, doing so, found herself suddenly facing the old parson, who had come up the street, and was standing there, looking at us all over the wall.

There was a noise of voices, telling him what was afoot, which died down abruptly, as he stared at us and said nothing.

Then Momphesson called to him across the churchyard, and across us all, 'Thomas Stanley! There is many a quarrel between thee and me, on doctrine, and on morals, and on faith. And yet I trust you, you being a man of God after your own lights, that you will stand at my side now, and help me, and tell the people that they must not go!'

Then there was a long moment while Parson Stanley drew breath ... and Parson Stanley said, 'Stir not any from this place. What good will it do you, to flee from the will of God? Is there a place of safety, if God wills your deaths? Or any danger if he wills it not? Stay where God has appointed you to dwell, and pray without cease!'

And at that, the frenzy ebbed from us, and left us feeling weak, and much distracted. Many of the women sat down suddenly upon the grass, or leaned their weight against the trees, or the gravestones. We could hear the wind sighing on the corners of the church-tower, and going on up the Edge; we could hear the water running in the brook near by.

Then Robert Wood said, 'Parson, granted that we do not take to our heels, and scatter to the ends of the country, still every day we come and go, fetching bread and flour from Hazleford Mill, forge-iron for the smithy, threads and needles, and fodder for cattle, much that we cannot have in Eyam, and cannot do without, unless we should starve. If the sickness clings to us invisible and may get to others in this way, might we not spread the sickness round the shire, just in our daily occasions?'

'We must bring all such traffic to a cease,' Parson Momphesson said.

'It will be very difficult to live, and full of hardship even for those who keep in health, if we do as you say, Parson,' my father said.

And Mary Heald went up to the parson, and plucked his sleeve, like a beggar woman bidding alms. 'We must go,' she said. 'Do not keep us; let us go!'

NOVEL: *A Parcel of Patterns*, Jill Paton Walsh

'I will not desert you,' he said. 'What help I can find, you shall have. We shall not lack the necessaries of life; I will appeal for what we need, to the Duke at Chatsworth and other worthies, and they will provide for us.'

'As have never done before, then!' cried out Marshall Howe. 'The lordly would damn their souls sooner than trouble over us!'

'But if the parson ask, for us . . .' murmured Mary Gregory.

'Let him try. Much good will it do!'

'Listen to me, Marshall Howe, and all,' said Momphesson. 'We will confine ourselves utterly within the parish bounds. And so I will promise the Duke. None shall cross the parish bounds, for life or death, until the Plague has run its course and departed from us. But where the roads cross the bound, we will use the boundary-stone to leave notes of requisition for all that we have need of, and the Duke will send us those things. His messengers will leave goods early in the morning, and we not come to take them till mid-day. I will most humbly ask him for this favour; but I will tell him that unless he help us, we cannot remain within Eyam bounds, and if we cannot . . .'

Reading and drama

There are ten named characters who speak in this extract, and Mal, the storyteller. There are also other unidentified villagers and many who respond as a group.

In small groups allocate parts and prepare a polished reading of this dramatic incident in the novel. You will need to:

- become familiar with a way of speaking no longer used. Take note of the punctuation and read the long speeches slowly;
- pick up the clues given about how each character responds to what both parsons say, e.g.
    'wailed Joaney Hodge'
    'quiet Robert Wood';
- decide how much of the narrative (story which is not dialogue) needs to be included so that the listener knows what Mal is thinking and feeling as she tells the story.

Picking up clues

Writing

Write an entry in your log-book recording your reading and discussion of the extract. Make use of the suggestions on page 11 and the example provided.

What helpful advice would you give to someone who might find difficulty in reading a challenging book? Jot down some useful notes.

DRAMA

The Silver Sword, Stuart Henson

Reading a play is not something you can do easily on your own and it certainly isn't as much fun as a lively group reading. Fortunately, in class you will have opportunities to work in small groups and to talk about what you have read.

You will find it easier to understand how plays work if you think about the problems facing the playwright:

- Not everything that people think, say or do can be written into a play script:
  - conversation and events are condensed into the time-scale of the play;
  - characters have to be 'suggested' rather than fully developed.
- *Silence* is an important part of the language of a play — how can this be used effectively?
- Stage directions and instructions to the actors and directors, to do with entrances, exits and movement around the set, have to be included. Sometimes it is necessary to give advice about a tone of voice or facial expression.
- The plot, the story of the action, must involve moments of tension, even in comedy.

The playwright also makes demands on his audience and his readers. Look at the following extract from the play of *The Silver Sword*. We must be prepared to 'believe', to enter into a partnership with the playwright and the actors, for us to accept that we can 'see' a street or be in a cellar, without having moved from our chairs.

Scene 2

The cellar. RUTH *and* BRONIA *set up box furniture* RUTH *sits and begins to match two tatty ends of curtain.* BRONIA *is rather sadly admiring her charcoal drawings which decorate the walls. One figure has a grin. She smudges out the grin and adds a 'sad' mouth. She turns to* RUTH.

BRONIA   What you doing with our sheets Ru?

RUTH   I want to make a cover for the gap in the wall. Edek will bring us better sheets anyway, and we've got to stop the draught somehow. [*To herself*] Trouble is I haven't got a needle. I suppose I'll have to make one from a splinter.

BRONIA is balancing a stick of charred wood on her fingers. Finally she drops it. She drags her feet over to where RUTH *is sitting and drapes her arms around* RUTH's *neck from behind.*

BRONIA   How long have we been living in this cellar Ruth?

RUTH   Don't know love – but look, at least we're safe here. The Nazis haven't got time to come searching across this side of the city for three lost kids.

Pause. BRONIA *moves away and sits on a box opposite* RUTH. *She bites her fingernails.*

RUTH [*a little sharp*]   Don't do that Bron!

BRONIA *starts to cry.*

RUTH [*exasperated*]   Oh Bronia, pull yourself together: I only *spoke* to you.

BRONIA   Please, Ruth, I don't know what to *do*. I'm fed up with this place. I don't like the rats. I want Mummy and Daddy to come back!

RUTH [*crosses to her*]   I'm sorry. I know it's not much fun for you. It's no joke for me either. Edek will be back soon. He's gone to the Polish Council to try to find out about Mum. [*She looks round rather hopelessly*] Why don't you do some more drawing?

BRONIA [*desperately*]   There's no more wall left Ru!

RUTH *sees this is true. She is moved by a surge of compassion for her little sister. She hugs* BRONIA *and swings her on to a box. She sits down next to her, confidentially.*

RUTH   I know what we'll do! We'll do what we always did. Starting tomorrow you are going to *school*!

BRONIA [*amazed*]   *Where* Ruth?

RUTH   Here, in this very room. We'll have our own school. Your friends from the street can come. I'm old enough to be your teacher. It'll do you all good. They can bomb every building in Warsaw, but it won't stop children learning how to add up and take away. And if there are no reading books ... well, we'll have to *tell* each other stories!

She begins to be carried away by her own ideas, pacing up and down the cellar. BRONIA *just sits and stares, wide-eyed.*

RUTH   We'll have lessons in the morning only. Plenty of time for play in the afternoon. We'll start with a Bible story – I shall have to remember carefully. Then arithmetic or writing. Then a break. We can do games and P.E. on the open site when there's not a raid –

EDEK *enters. She stops abruptly. There is a silence.*

EDEK [*forced cheerfulness*]   I got some bread at the convent. [*Silence*] And I fixed up a job at the soup-kitchen one of the boys was run in for theft ... [*He breaks off*]

RUTH   Edek!

He can hide it no longer. He sits C. looking up at audience. RUTH *and* BRONIA *move to him.*

EDEK   They said Mum was taken to Germany to work on the land. But they can't say where.

Blackout 5 seconds.

Scene 3

JOSEPH [*narrator*]   In the summer they left the city for the woods. Life was healthier there. They lived under an oak tree. When it rained, they got wet. When the sun shone it browned their limbs.

Because of the kindness of the peasants, food was more plentiful. It was forbidden to store food or to sell to anyone but the Nazis, but they gave the children whatever they could spare.

They hid it too, in cellars, in haystacks, in holes in the ground. With the help of the older children they smuggled it to the towns and sold it on the black market. Edek was a good smuggler. Ruth and Bronia were well fed, for he was well paid.

Improvisation VII EDEK *barters with* PEASANT 2 *over barrow-load of filled logs which he is to take to the* PEASANT*'s accomplice in the market; ends with* EDEK *forcing price up.*

PEASANT 2 O.K. O.K. You're good. It's dangerous. Two rye loaves, apples and butter. Under the cattle trough in the top field tomorrow. Leave the cart in the first barn.

They shake hands on it. Exit PEASANT. EDEK *pushes away barrow to C., stops and turns to audience.*

EDEK At school they taught me how to
Play the game
Follow the rules
'Honest' was my middle name

But now I know the two-faced world
More than I did before
Some rules are only for the rich
And others for the poor

To those who have, to them
Shall all the more be given
God bless the helpless
Their reward's in heaven!

Don't tell me that I'm cheating now
I know the score:
Trust yourself, trust no-one else:
Their game is war.

EDEK *pushes the barrow round in a circle. As he returns he meets a crowd – the market.* TWO GERMAN SOLDIERS *enter* R. EDEK *whistling, almost runs into them.*

SOLDIER 1 'Ello what 'ave we 'ere then?

SOLDIER 2 Goin' somewhere, young man?

SOLDIER 1 Anythin' to declare?

SOLDIER 2 Anythin' we ought to know about?

SOLDIER 1 Got a pretty sister at 'ome?

SOLDIER 2 Get on wiv me mate would she?

SOLDIER 1 What's on yer wagon mate?

SOLDIER 2 Logs in summer?

SOLDIER 1 Suspicious!

SOLDIER 2 Most suspicious!

SOLDIER 1 'Ave a look shall we?

SOLDIER 2 Wouldn't be tryin' t' pull a fast one eh?

SOLDIER 1 Stop us seein' the wood for the trees?

SOLDIERS begin to examine the logs. EDEK is off, like a rabbit. He dodges among the crowd who obstruct the SOLDIERS. He makes his escape up the audience steps R. The SOLDIERS stop at the bottom.

SOLDIER 1 'E's got away!

SOLDIER 2 Yeh – I know 'im 'e's slippery as an eel. But I got 'im marked down – we'll get 'im next time.

They disappear into shadow, audience R.

Scene 4

Cellar interior: RUTH *is standing before the 'class' of ragged school children.*

RUTH So although the king knew he had been tricked, he had to go through with it. He called for Daniel and sent him into the den. And he rolled a huge stone over the entrance of the den and sealed it himself. Then he went back to his palace, but he couldn't sleep, thinking about Daniel, wondering if the lions would devour him.

  Well, when morning came, he rushed out and rolled back the stone and there stood Daniel, all in one piece, with the lions dozing quietly around him. And Daniel said: 'O King live forever, my God has sent an angel who shut the lions' mouths and they have not hurt me'.

  She stops, sighs, satisfied.

EVA [*after a pause*] Please Ruth – Miss – are you going to tell us what the story means?

Others murmur 'Yes – you always tell us . . . etc.

RUTH Why don't you tell me, Eva? Your meaning is as good as anyone else's.

EVA *looks down at her feet.*

RUTH [*smiles*] Don't worry, Eva. [*Pause*] Well, sometimes I think of it as the story of our own troubles. The lions are: cold and hunger and hardship. But if only we are patient and trustful like Daniel, we will be delivered from them . . .
[*she falters*]
Sometimes though I see the lions scowling and snarling. . . . [*snapping out of it*], No! never mind that. We've been in this damp cellar too long this morning. Out you go everybody: into the sun!

Improvisation VIII: *The children play 'Air-raid alert'* RUTH *remains in cellar C. While attention is focused on game* JAN *drags himself close to edge of stage – Audience L. and collapses unseen.*

BRONIA [*runs towards* JAN, *sees him, stops, approaches him cautiously. After a pause*] Ruth, Ruth, there's a boy lying down outside and he won't get up.

RUTH Tickle his ribs!

BRONIA I don't think he can get up.

RUTH Who is it?

BRONIA It's not one of the class. I've never seen him before.

RUTH *goes to investigate.*

RUTH [*to the children who have gathered round*] Does anyone know who he is? [*They shake their heads.*]

RUTH He looks ill and starved. Yankel, will you help me lift him down to the cellar? And Eva, please find something for him to drink, some milk if you can get it.

They move him to C.
JAN *calls for his pet* 'Where's Jimpy?' *One of the children fetches a crate with the cockerel from* JAN'S *point of entrance.*
JAN *calls the name again.*

RUTH That's a fine name, what's yours?

EVA *returns with cup.*

RUTH All right you others, I think this young man needs a rest. Off you go and play again. [*They do so reluctantly*].

Picking up clues

[*To* JAN] Look, Eva's brought some milk for you. Sit up and drink it. You'll feel better in a minute.

JAN *sits up and drinks.* BRONIA *comes back, whispers to* RUTH.

BRONIA [*to others*]   He still won't tell us his name!

KATE [*brings* JAN'*s box from Audience L.*]   I found this in the street where he was lying. I think it must be his.

BRONIA [*snatching box*]   It's heavy and it rattles. He must be rich! Ruth, may we undo the string?

RUTH [*with authority*]   Give the box to him. Nobody shall touch it without asking him.

JAN *takes the box and smiles. The children clamour to find out what's inside.*

JAN [*holding the box out of reach*]   No-one sees into my treasure box. But since you gave it back to me I'll tell you my name. It's Jan.

RUTH [*holds out her hand*]   I'm Ruth, this is my sister Bronia. These children are from the street. They go to our school. [JAN *looks puzzled*] We live here in the cellar. There used to be three of us, but my brother Edek went out smuggling one day and never came back.

She looks across to Audience Right where EDEK *appears momentarily and is arrested by the* TWO SOLDIERS *who have been waiting in the shadows. They search him and discover food being smuggled inside his coat.*

RUTH   Perhaps you will help us find him again. Perhaps now you have come we shall be lucky.

Lights to half on stage. Spot upon JOSEPH, *narrator.*

JOSEPH   For some days Jan was too ill to leave. What he needed was rest, warmth and good solid food. Ruth was a good nurse. The children left him alone, but they scrounged for him what they could for food. By the time Jan was better he didn't want to go.

Edek had gone; Jan had arrived. The Germans went; the Russians arrived. Several streets away there appeared a brand new hut – a Russian control post. . . .

Reading   On a first reading it might be a good idea to ask one of your group to be responsible for reading all the *essential*

DRAMA: *The Silver Sword*, Stuart Henson

stage directions. Individual characters should be able to pick up the clues about how they should interpret their parts.

Talking and note-making

- Talk about what we learn from *the dialogue* about:
  - the characters;
  - their relationship to each other; and
  - the situation they are in.
- What extra information is given in the stage directions?
- Why do you think the playwright invites the actors to develop the drama without the help of a script at two points in these scenes?
- Discuss the role of the narrator. If you have read the novel, you will know that Joseph is the children's father.
- What advantage or disadvantage is there in having Joseph as the narrator for these particular scenes?
- Why are the two German soldiers introduced at the end of Scene Three? Talk about the ways in which their conversation is different from that of the other characters.
- In what ways are *pauses* and silences used to add to the dramatic effectiveness of these scenes?
- At which point in Scene Four does the playwright withhold some information from his characters that the audience already knows? What does this add to the scene?
- Your discussion should have helped you to enjoy a second, more thoughtful reading of all the scenes.

Drama

Work in groups. Choose one of the scenes to develop as a dramatic presentation. You might like to appoint a director for this piece of work.

- Cast the scene. Make use of your notes and discussion about characters. Encourage lines to be learned as soon as is reasonable.

    If you choose a scene which uses improvisation, let everyone in the group contribute ideas. Try out several before deciding which movement and speech seems natural and flows easily back into the play script.
- Plan and draw a diagram of the set. You will need to decide how best to make use of available floor space and/or stage area.

- Plot exits, entrances and essential movement within the acting area after discussion with the cast.
- Collect essential props.
- Rehearse your individual scenes. You may be able to link all three scenes together to share with another class about to read the book. Your presentation could be followed by a discussion through which you should discover how successful your audience has been in 'picking up clues'.

VERSE

Picking up clues in poetry

There are as many ways of 'reading' and responding to poetry as there are poems to be read.

In this section, we suggest a few approaches for you to try which will help you to become more confident readers and writers of poems. Keep the following in mind.
- Poetry should be *heard* as well as *seen*. It should be read aloud, since it is concerned with sound, rhythm, metre and language.
- Most poems require reading several times and returning to at regular intervals over a long period of time because they often convey important ideas or opinions in a very few words which cannot be fully understood in one reading.
- Compiling your own anthology gives you a chance to become familiar with those poems which you have enjoyed. It is a good idea to keep them in a file so that you can, in the future, add other poems on a similar theme or by the same poet. Your own written work could accompany that of the poets.
- Talking about a poem in pairs or small groups is one of the most helpful and interesting ways of exploring the ideas in it. But be prepared for not understanding immediately what the poem is about and try not to ask yourself whether you *like* it. This kind of talk *closes* a discussion before it has had a chance to develop.

VERSE: Picking up clues in poetry

Here are some 'stepping stones' to guide you through your discussions.

1. Forget about the meaning of the poem and whether you like it or not.

2. Give particular attention to the title; the poet will have chosen this with care.

3. Read the poem several times very slowly. Try to hear the poem aloud in your head. Pay close attention to punctuation.

4. Jot down any unusual or forceful words or phrases which capture your attention.

5. Group together any words or phrases which seem to you to be connected in any way.

6. Now look at your notes. Can you see a pattern taking shape? Are you able to use the clues to make connections?

7. Read the poem again. Talk your way through possible meanings referring to appropriate parts of the poem.

Talk around the following questions. Jot down notes to help you with any writing or reporting you may be required to do.

- Who is 'speaking' the poem? Is it the poet or a person, creature or object created by the poet to speak for him/her? Is there more than one 'voice' in the poem?
- To whom is the poet 'speaking'? Is it to a particular person, e.g. a daughter, the whole of humanity, or to him/herself?
- What feelings and attitudes are being expressed by the poet and/or 'speaker' in the poem? Are they angry,

Picking up clues

sarcastic, passionate, respectful, full of wonder, light-hearted, teasing?
- Why has the poet arranged the poem in the way it appears?
- Are you now able to share your understanding of the poem, using all your notes?
- Are there any other questions you would like to ask about the poem? Jot them down.

Scafell Pike, Norman Nicholson

We asked one second-year group to read the following poem by Norman Nicholson. First, the poem:

Look
Along the well
Of the street,
Between the gasworks and the neat
Sparrow-stepped gable
Of the Catholic chapel,
High
Above tilt and crook
Of the tumbledown
Roofs of the town –
Scafell Pike,
The tallest hill in England.

How small it seems,
So far away,
No more than a notch
On the plate-glass window of the sky!
Watch
A puff of kitchen smoke
Block out peak and pinnacle –
Rock-pie of volcanic lava
Half a mile thick
Scotched out
At the click of an eye.

VERSE: *Scafell Pike*, Norman Nicholson

Brainstorming the title before reading the poem

Pike – fish?
fell – something knocked down
Scafell Pike – a dead fish?
         – the name of something?
         – the name of somebody in a legend?

Interesting features of the poem

– the narrow shape of the poem
– only two full stops in the whole poem
– several run-on lines

Striking words and phrases

– Look, High, Watch
– Sparrow-stepped gable
– Above tilt and crook
– notch
– plate-glass window of the sky
– pinnacle
– Rock-pie
– Scotched out
– click of an eye

Word boxes

Along	Look
Between	High
Above	Watch

Above	street
Scafell Pike	gasworks
tallest hill	chapel
peak and pinnacle	Roofs
volcanic lava	smoke

Picking up clues

Talking and writing

Work in small groups. Are there any other possibilities you would like to add to those already suggested?

Work on steps 6 and 7 and jot down your answers to the questions on pages 27–8.

Share your thoughts about this poem with other groups.

Drawing

Draw or describe two pictures (one for each stanza) to capture the *images*, the *perspective* and *feelings* as expressed by the poet.

If you live in the North-West part of England, you would have known immediately what the poem was going to be about. But by following the approach we have suggested, you should have a closer understanding and appreciation of *how* and *why* Norman Nicholson wrote the poem in the way he did. This way of working should help you to read and discuss more difficult poems.

Now choose another poem from this or any other book and explore it using the guidelines set out in this chapter.

Here are some more ideas for you to enjoy using in groups.

Filling in the gaps

A Child Half-(—)

Stealthily parting the small-hours silence,
a hardly-embodied figment of his brain
comes down to (—) with me
as I work late.
Flat-footed, as though his (—) and feet
were still asleep.

On a stool,
staring into the fire,
his dummy dangling.
Fire (—) the small coals of his eyes;
it (—) back through the holes
into his head, into the darkness.

I ask what (—) him.

'A wolf (—) me,' he says.

VERSE: *Scafell Pike*, Norman Nicholson

Reading and talking
- Read the poem several times. Talk about and jot down all the possible words for each gap.
- Ring round the ones you think most appropriate and give reasons for your choices.
- Look on page 32 to see the words the poet used and comment on his choice.

Sequencing

The following list is made up of twenty-three scrambled segments from a poem by A.P. Herbert.

1   In short, foul woman, it would suit
2   If you keep shouting who it is
3   But, let me tell you, I do not.
    The author seeks to keep from me
4   Don't breathe upon my neck so much.
5   Since you have just foretold it all.
    The lady you have brought with you.
6   I never saw it till today
7   I understand, in some surprise;
8   Me just as well if you were mute;
    In fact to make my meaning plain,
9   The actors in their funny way
10 Dear Madam, you have seen this play;
11 I trust you will not speak again.
12 And you are not a friend of his
13 If you have said them just before
14 But I can understand the piece
15 But they do not amuse me more
16 You know the details of the plot,
17 And – may I add one human touch? –
18 Have several funny things to say,
19 Without assistance from your niece
20 The murderer's identity
21 Is, I infer, a half-wit too,
22 The merit of the drama lies
23 But the surprise must now be small

Clues: The title is: *At the Theatre – To the lady behind me.*
It is written as one stanza, in rhymed couplets.

31

Picking up clues

Talking and writing

Rearrange these lines so that they make a poem. When you have finished, look below at the original poem. Jot down and talk about:
- any differences between your draft and that of the poet;
- your method of working;
- what you have learned from working in this way.

Asking questions

Each group is allowed to ask a maximum of *two* questions that are left unanswered when the poem you are discussing has been explored. The one or two significant questions may then be put to another group to answer.

Poster poems

An interesting way of responding to a poem is to draw the images suggested by a close reading. It need not be a finished piece of impressive art work; the intention is to capture the essence of the poem in your drawing.

Giving your work to another pupil who has not read the poem will provide the basis for a discussion about the *ideas* in the poem, not the skill of your drawing.

Solutions

A Child Half-<u>asleep</u>   by Tony Connor

sit, legs, ignites, stares, woke, dreamed

At the Theatre

To the lady behind me

Dear Madam, you have seen this play;
I never saw it till today.
You know the details of the plot,
But, let me tell you, I do not.

VERSE: *Scafell Pike,* Norman Nicholson

The author seeks to keep from me
The murderer's identity,
And you are not a friend of his
If you keep shouting who it is.
The actors in their funny way
Have several funny things to say,
But they do not amuse me more
If you have said them just before.
The merit of the drama lies,
I understand, in some surprise;
But the surprise must now be small
Since you have just foretold it all.
The lady you have brought with you
Is, I infer, a half-wit too,
But I can understand the piece
Without assistance from your niece.
In short, foul woman, it would suit
Me just as well if you were mute;
In fact, to make my meaning plain,
I trust you will not speak again.
And – may I add one human touch? –
Don't breathe upon my neck so much.

2 Finding your voice and finding a focus

STORYTELLING

I Like to Stay Up, Grace Nichols

I like to stay up
and listen
when big people talking
jumbie stories

Oooooooooooooooooh
I does feel so tingly
and excited
inside – eeeeeeeeeee

But when my mother say
'Girl, time for bed'
then is when
I does feel a dread
then is when
I does jump into me bed
then is when
I does cover up
from me feet to me head

then is when
I does wish
I didn't listen
to no stupid jumbie story
then is when
I does wish
I did read me book instead

In this delightful poem, Grace Nichols has captured an experience many of us have shared. Do you remember, as a young child, any occasions when you listened in on adults telling stories about members of the family, local happenings, unusual and perhaps frightening events? Were there any stories that you enjoyed hearing over and over again?

Listening to stories and telling our own is one of the most important ways through which we become better at talking, reading and writing.

Professor Harold Rosen has written a great deal about the value of story-making. In the following extract he tells us about one of his own childhood memories of family storytelling.

A Story for Every Item, Harold Rosen

My mother had a black trunk which she bought for the sea journey back to England from America. It became in our household a grand piece of furniture even though it was kept under her bed. I have it still. Inside, it had two layers, the top one was a deep tray one half of which had a lid. Once its travelling function was finished the trunk was used as a storage unit for all the family photographs, hundreds of them, lying pell-mell in the lower section. The tray held an assortment of documents and mementoes, the lidded section being reserved for precious sentimental objects. From time to time my mother had some need, real or pretended, to seek out some paper or other from the trunk – a birth certificate, a letter, a membership card, a newspaper cutting. At such moments she would sit on the floor by the open trunk and my sister and I would sit by her. The ritual was unfailing. Every photo, every document, every object was inspected and for each one there was its proper story. There were relatives in Durban and Johannesburg, in Rochester and Philadelphia, in Strasbourg, and in Warsaw and Vienna. How did uncles, aunts, cousins, two brothers and a father come to be scattered over the face of the earth? Why were some of the men in uniform wearing the uniform of the wrong side? Who was alive and who was dead? Why was the ostrich feather fan so precious to her? The miniature replica of a miner's lamp, what did that signify? Who was Eugene Debs whose bronze bust wrapped in tissue paper lodged in the covered section of the tray? Who married whom? Whose children were they? Who died young and how? Who lived in that house? What happened, what happened, what happened? A story for every item.

And we all have stories to tell all our lives.

Story by a first-year pupil

This is a story told by a first-year pupil at an East London school:

About a year ago my friend told me about this railway man, he used to work on top of the arches at Millwall Park, and he got killed by the trains. I didn't believe him at the time, 'cos I didn't know where he'd got the information from. One night I was coming back from football practice, from Millwall Youth, and it was about eight-ish, between eight and nine o'clock, and I was on a bike with me mate, right? We was just going under the tunnel when we heard some footsteps going along – they was tapping and tapping – and we looked round and we saw the shadow of a lantern on the wall of the arches. We got a bit scared so we went a bit faster, and then we heard drums tapping – you know, drums: boom, boom, boom, boom – and they got really faster, and faster and faster. Then, when we got home we never went to the arches again, we always left early.

Talking and reading

■ Re-read the three examples of storytelling. Look at our notes:

STORYTELLING: Story by a first-year pupil

I Like to Stay Up

Child	Adults
– listening, late at night, possibly only half-understanding – hearing stories from past culture – enjoying being afraid	– telling stories about spirits, ghosts, unnatural events – sharing stories of their own culture – accepting the child as a listener – adults enjoying story-telling

A Story for Every Item

Children	Mother
– enjoying a ritual – finding a link with their past – asking questions – learning more about their mother	– recalling her past – handling treasured possessions – showing feelings

This railway man . . .

Friend telling	Friend listening
– re-telling a story handed on – first hand experience of the event – experience of being a storyteller – expects to be listened to	– enjoys the drama in the story – knows he has a story to tell if he listens carefully! – is willing to listen and encourage the storyteller

- Talk about the value of these three experiences to the *storytellers* as well as to the *listeners*.
- What indications are there in the third story that it is being *told*, not written down?
    - If the story had to be written, what changes or additions would you make?
    - Would you write in the third person or keep the story in the first person?
    - How would you manage to convey the excitement and tension in the story if it became a written account?
- Write a ghost story, making use of the incident in the third story if you wish.
- Exchange stories about a memorable incident, photograph or object. If possible, tape-record some of your stories.

37

Finding your voice and finding a focus

- Re-tell one of the stories you have been told, to a third person. You would find it interesting if you taped both the 'tellings' and talked about any differences.

THE WRITER'S VOICE
A Letter from Bhavana

It is very important that when we write our stories we do not leave out the 'voice' of the storyteller; it is that personal quality in the writing which makes it powerful. Young children seem to be able to write very naturally in their own 'voices'.

An outstanding young writer who seems to be 'talking' to her very dear uncle is this six-year-old girl.

> 7th June 76
>
> My so very dearly dear Uncle,
>
> I bet this letter is going to meet you with quite a surprise when you find out who it is from. I shouldn't really reveal my name and better leave it to you to guess who I am. I can not make up my mind whether I should or whether I shouldn't tell you my name. Never mind, I have decided not to keep you in any more suspense any longer. Here I am right out with my name, Bhavana. I do hope that you have not forgot me. I say so because we have not met each other for quite a long time.

THE WRITER'S VOICE: A Letter from Bhavana

Uncle, I am not too well today. I have got some cold that I caught from Alika the other day. Hers went better and mine went worse. So she is off to school while I am off it. I was getting fed up and decided to do a letter to you. I miss you a lot because you are a very very nice uncle. I know I am very shy in front of you but I am getting over it slowly. but surely I hope you won't find me as shy as you did last time.

Uncle, I have turned out to be a left hander after all which I believe is pretty unusual for a Indian girl. But I'm sorry I just couldn't help. My mammy and daddy tried very hard to stop me from using my left hand for writing and eating. I try quite a lot still to see if I can ever get used to my right hand and give my parents and my sister a pleasant surprise. But I don't think I can win. I'll keep trying though.

Uncle, I'll be 7 next October. You will be glad to read that I have already finished about 20 books in reading at school. When we were in Rainhill, I was always ahead of everybody in the class. I always loved to go to school there because it was such a lovely school. But this new school that I have now gone to is not a good one. It gives me tummy ache when I think of it. Phaps that is why I don't keep well. I miss my old friend Johanne in the other school who was always so good to me. My daddy already knows that I don't like going to this new school very much. So he is sending me to a Public School as soon as I get a seat there. I hope I should be O.K. then. My daddy is awfully nice to me and never shouts at me.

Uncle, I don't really like our new house but it's quite big and roomy. My daddy has spent an awful lot of money on it. He has made it look quite nice really. We have got central heating put in and carpets all over. I am sure you will like it when you come over to see us. It's a long long time since you have been here last. It seems ages, it really does.

THE WRITER'S VOICE: *A Letter from Bhavana*

> uncle, I love to go on and on and hate to finish. But I'm afraid I have got to do so because there is no more lines left. And also I'm getting late for my dinner. My daddy is in the kitchen and he's shouting like mad. I will write a lot lot more next time. Please do ignore my mistakes. Bhavana

Through her writing, Bhavana is doing much more than passing time during absence from school.

Talking

- Discuss what you learn about the child and her family from her letter.
- What examples are there in her letter to show that she is able to look at things from another person's point of view?
- Discuss the importance of the letter to the child and to her uncle.

As you develop your reading and writing, you may find yourself imitating other 'voices', other writers. When asked to write a story or a poem, you might immediately think of something you have read by somebody else on the same feeling or topic. This could help you to become a more confident reader and writer. It is important, however, that you do not lose your own 'voice' and ideas.

I Can't Write No Pretty Poem, Toni Cade

Many of us have felt the same kind of frustration expressed by the next writer:

As she headed down the hall to her next class, Geraldine remembered that she hadn't done the homework for English. Mrs Scott had said to write a poem, and Geraldine had meant to do it at lunchtime. After all, there was nothing to it – a flower here, a raindrop there, moon, June, rose, nose. But the men carrying off the furniture had made her forget.

'And now put away your books,' Mrs Scott was saying as Geraldine tried to scribble a poem quickly. 'Today we can give King Arthur's Knights a rest. Let's talk about poetry.'

Mrs Scott moved up and down the aisles, talking about her favourite poems and reciting a line now and then. She got very excited whenever she passed a desk and could pick up the homework from a student who had remembered to do the assignment.

'A poem is your own special way of saying what you feel and what you see,' Mrs Scott went on, her lips moist. It was her favourite subject.

'Some poets write about the light that ... that ... makes the world sunny,' she said, passing Geraldine's desk. 'Sometimes an idea takes the form of a picture – an image.'

For almost half an hour Mrs Scott stood at the front of the room, reading poems and talking about the lives of the great poets. Geraldine drew more houses and designs for curtains.

'So for those who haven't done their homework, try it now,' Mrs Scott said. 'Try expressing what it is like to be ... to be alive in this ... this glorious world.'

'Oh, brother,' Geraldine muttered to herself as Mrs Scott moved up and down the aisles again, waving her hands and leaning over the student's shoulders and saying, 'That's nice,' or 'Keep trying'. Finally she came to Geraldine's desk and stopped, looking down at her.

THE WRITER'S VOICE: *I Can't Write No Pretty Poem*, Toni Cade

'I can't write a poem,' Geraldine said flatly, before she even realised she was going to speak at all. She said it very loudly and the whole class looked up.

'And why not?' Mrs Scott asked, looking hurt.

'I can't write a poem, Mrs Scott, because nothing lovely's been happening in my life. I haven't seen a flower since Mother's Day, and the sun don't even shine on my side of the street. No robins come sing on my window sill.'

Geraldine swallowed hard. She thought about saying that her father doesn't even come to visit any more, but changed her mind. 'Just the rain comes,' she went on, 'and the bills come, and the men to move out our furniture. I'm sorry, but I can't write no pretty poem.'

Teddy Johnson leaned over and was about to giggle and crack the whole class up, but Mrs Scott looked so serious that he changed his mind.

'You have just said the most ... the most poetic thing, Geraldine Moore,' said Mrs Scott. Her hands flew up to touch the silk scarf around her neck. ' "Nothing lovely's been happening in my life." ' She repeated it so quietly that everyone had to lean forward to hear.

'Class,' Mrs Scott said very sadly, clearing her throat. 'You have just heard the best poem you will ever hear.' She went to the board and stood there for a long time staring at the chalk in her hand.

'I'd like you to copy it down,' she said. She wrote it just as Geraldine had said it, bad grammar and all.

Nothing lovely's been happening in my life.
I haven't seen a flower since Mother's Day,
And the sun don't even shine on my side of the street.
No robins come sing on my window sill
Just the rain comes, and the bills come,
And the men to move out our furniture.
I'm sorry, but I can't write no pretty poem.

Mrs Scott stopped writing, but she kept her back to the class for a long time – long after Geraldine had closed her notebook.

And even when the bell rang and everyone came over to smile at Geraldine or to tap her on the shoulder or to kid her about being the school poet, Geraldine waited for Mrs Scott to put the chalk down and turn around. Finally Geraldine stacked up her books and started to leave.

Bridge to Terabithia, Katherine Paterson

In the following extract from *Bridge to Terabithia,* Leslie Burke has managed to write about her hobby in such a way that the whole class is interested and impressed.

It started with Mrs. Myers reading out loud a composition that Leslie had written about her hobby. Everyone had had to write a paper about his or her favorite hobby. Jess had written about football, which he really hated, but he had enough brains to know that if he said drawing, everyone would laugh at him. Most of the boys swore that watching the Washington Redskins on TV was their favorite hobby. The girls were divided: those who didn't care much about what Mrs. Myers thought chose watching game shows on TV, and those like Wanda Kay Moore who were still aiming for A's chose reading Good Books. But Mrs. Myers didn't read anyone's paper out loud except Leslie's.

"I want to read this composition aloud. For two reasons. One, it is *beautifully* written. And two, it tells about an unusual hobby – for a girl." Mrs. Myers beamed her first-day smile at Leslie. Leslie stared at her desk. Being Mrs. Myers' pet was pure poison at Lark Creek. "'Scuba Diving' by Leslie Burke."

Mrs. Myers' sharp voice cut Leslie's sentences into funny little phrases, but even so, the power of Leslie's words drew Jess with her under the dark water. Suddenly he could hardly breathe. Suppose you went under and your mask filled all up with water and you couldn't get to the top in time? He was choking and sweating. He tried to push down his panic. This was Leslie Burke's favorite hobby. Nobody would make up scuba diving to be their favorite hobby if it wasn't so. That meant Leslie did it a lot. That she wasn't scared of going deep, deep down in a world of no air and little light. Lord, he was such a coward. How could he be all in a tremble just listening to Mrs. Myers read about it? He was worse a baby than Joyce Ann. His dad expected him to be a man. And here he was letting some girl who wasn't even ten yet scare the liver out of him by just telling what it was like to sight-see under water. Dumb, dumb, dumb.

"I am sure," Mrs. Myers was saying, "that all of you were as impressed as I was with Leslie's exciting essay."

Impressed. Lord. He'd nearly drowned.

In the classroom there was a shuffling of feet and papers. "Now I want to give you a homework assignment" – muffled groans – "that I'm sure you'll enjoy." – mumblings of unbelief – "Tonight on Channel 7 at 8 P.M. there is going to be a special about a famous underwater explorer – Jacques Cousteau. I want everyone to watch. Then write one page telling what you learned."

"A whole page?"

"Yes."

"Does spelling count?"

"Doesn't spelling always count, Gary?"

"Both sides of the paper?"

"One side will be enough, Wanda Kay. But I will give extra credit to those who do extra work."

Wanda Kay smiled primly. You could already see ten pages taking shape in her pointy head.

"Mrs. Myers."

"Yes, Leslie." Lord, Mrs. Myers was liable to crack her face if she kept up smiling like that.

"What if you can't watch the program?"

"You inform your parents that it is a homework assignment. I am sure they will not object."

"What if" – Leslie's voice faltered; then she shook her head and cleared her throat so the words came out stronger – "what if you don't have a television set?"

Lord, Leslie. Don't say that. You can always watch on mine. But it was too late to save her. The hissing sounds of disbelief were already building into a rumbling of contempt.

Mrs. Myers blinked her eyes. "Well. Well." She blinked some more. You could tell she was trying to figure out how to save Leslie, too. "Well. In that case one could write a one-page composition on something else. Couldn't one, Leslie?" She tried to smile across the classroom upheaval to Leslie, but it was no use. "Class! Class! *Class!*" Her Leslie smile shifted suddenly and ominously into a scowl that silenced the storm.

Finding your voice and finding a focus

Talking and writing

- Read the extracts several times so that you have a close understanding of how each young writer feels and how each teacher responds.
- Look back to the notes we made on page 37. Using this method, or any other that helps you to 'see' what you are thinking, make notes which sum up what is happening in each case and what has been learned. We have given you one example.

Geraldine What is happening?	*Geraldine* What is learned?
– forgot to do her homework – thinks writing poetry is easy – thinks poetry has to be about flowers and raindrops, etc. – has family problems – is feeling unhappy and insecure – draws houses and curtains all the time Mrs. Scott is talking – finally expresses what she is thinking and feeling by *talking* out loud	– that poetry is 'your own special way of saying what you feel and what you see' – that she has something to say – that the teacher can help her to express her feelings in writing by shaping her spoken words – poetry doesn't have to rhyme – she has learned to accept praise and teasing from other pupils – that teachers have feelings!

Mrs. Scott What is happening?	*Mrs. Scott* What is learned?
– excited and enthusiastic about her favourite subject – talks for half an hour! – is unaware of Geraldine's lack of attention – sets the pupil a task: 'Try expressing what it is like to be alive in this glorious world' – walks around encouraging individual pupils – is 'hurt' when Geraldine says that she can't write a poem – listens carefully when Geraldine explains	– that if poetry is about saying what you feel and what you see in your own special way, then 'poets' must choose what they want to write about – the importance of talking to her pupils whilst they are writing – the importance of listening carefully to what Geraldine is struggling to express – that it is not always appropriate to correct everything in the first draft – that Geraldine has found her 'voice'

THE WRITER'S VOICE: *Bridge to Terabithia*, Katherine Paterson

Mrs. Scott What is happening? (continued)	
– immediately recognises a poem when she hears one – uses the opportunity to teach the whole class what speech can look like when written down as a poem – she is moved by the whole experience	

Now that you have thought about the pupil writer in each of the two extracts, jot down:
- any of your own writing experiences that you are reminded of through reading about other pupils' difficulties;
- what conditions help you to concentrate on a writing task;
- how you generally prepare yourself for writing – do you talk through your ideas with anyone else?
- a list of all the different kinds of writing and reading that you do in an average week at school and at home;
- how you decide what 'form' your writing should take, e.g. letter, list of instructions, story, etc.
- what help you think you need to become a better writer.

Share your ideas with the rest of the class. You will probably find that you have lots of common experiences and might even discover new ways of helping each other over particular difficulties.

How I Started Writing for Children,
Gillian Cross and Betsy Byars

Two modern authors writing for pupils of your age describe how they first started writing and some of the problems they encountered. First of all, Gillian Cross:

I was nearly thirty when I wrote my first book. It seems extraordinary, now, that it took me so long to begin. Even when I was eight or nine, I used to invent titles for novels and write myself glowing reviews in my head. The actual books were beyond me (how did anyone write so many *words?*) but I practised for my future as An Author by writing self-conscious, arty little descriptions – when I could escape from making up cowboy stories to entertain my little brother.

At secondary school, as befitted a Budding Writer, I specialised in English Literature. And how daunting it was. All those metaphors and similes! The characterisation! The symbolism! How did anyone cram all those into a novel and still manage to tell a story?

My own attempts to write became stilted, never progressing beyond Chapter One, and I kept them secret from my friends – amusing them, instead, with an interminable serial story of which they were the heroines. I told it on the train journey home, making it up as I went along.

At University, I was still an Eng. Lit. student, and growing anxious, because it was time to stop Budding and start Writing Seriously. But by now I could hardly get past Page One of anything I began. The more I studied, the more I understood the importance of every word. The nuances. The patterns of sound. The differences in register. Altering and re-altering my own skimpy efforts. I wondered how anyone developed a style like the ones I analysed in my tutorials. It was a relief to forget the whole business and go home in the evening. There was no time

THE WRITER'S VOICE: *How I Started Writing for Children*, Gillian Cross

to worry about my ambitions while I was playing with my little son, or telling him stories. He liked to hear his favourites over and over again. I particularly remember one I made up about a little blue car. After telling it every evening for a month, I knew the final, polished version by heart.

... then Betsy Byars:

Betsy Byars did not always want to be a writer. 'At school I had absolutely no interest in writing. I liked the outdoor life; I thought writers must have the most boring life in the world, sitting and typing all day by themselves. Now that's just what I do; but I have never been bored. I have been frustrated, disappointed, happy and flat; but I have *never* been bored.'

*

Her writing now feeds off observation and memory, not least memories of her own childhood.

*

Many of Betsy Byars' characters live rich fantasy lives inside their heads. As she talks about one of her own childhood pleasures you feel that's another thing they might share. 'I could already read quite well when I started school. I admired my older sister very much – she was a good reader so I suppose I wanted to be like her. I loved books with chapters – if a book didn't have chapters it had no value for me at all.

*

Straight from College she married Ed who had a University post teaching Engineering. 'We had two daughters almost straight away and a very happy young faculty social life.' Then Ed decided to take his PhD. 'We went to Illinois where I knew nobody. We lived in a barracks apartment. Everyone else was taking courses, working, doing something. I was there by myself with my kids.' That was the turning point. 'I had always thought maybe I would try writing some day. Now was the ideal opportunity. It was a case of "I know I can write something but I don't know what it is going to be!" So I tried everything: magazine articles, mystery stories (I loved reading mysteries so I thought that might be it, but it didn't work out).

*

The important thing was having the children around. 'There's a big gap between adults and kids. We forget totally what it is like to be ten. My kids were very communicative. When they came home from school and told me what had happened or what they were worried about it would make me remember things that had happened to me and how I'd felt. I'm sure I would not have written what I've written if I had not had kids. There would have been no way.'

*

'I've always loved odd things. I go through life storing them up consciously and unconsciously for future use.' A friend of her daughter, seeing two cobwebs on the ceiling, climbed on the piano stool and did an impression of Tarzan swinging. 'Only a child would make that association. An adult would see the cobwebs and think, "that ceiling is dirty." She used that happening obliquely. In *The Eighteenth Emergency* Mouse is lying on his back. Seeing some cobwebs, he draws an arrow on the wall and writes 'Unsafe for Swinging'. 'That incident opened up all of Mouse's personality to me.'

That exemplifies the way Betsy Byars writes – exploring the characters and what they will do. 'It takes me a long time to do a first draft. I don't know where I'm going when I start out. I come to halts and just have to pause and wait. It doesn't always work out as I planned it.

*

'Once I get a first draft and I know it's a book, it's just total pleasure adding to it. I don't do any sequels so there's always the feeling that this is the only time I'm ever going to write about these people. I want everyone to know everything I want them to know. They are all very real to me. It wouldn't surprise me at all if one of them came up and said "I'm Ezzie, I was in your book." I see them perfectly, so clearly. That's why I don't describe them.'

With all the humour, Betsy Byars' characters find

themselves facing some big issues: death, their own and others, bullying, emotional deprivation, fear, conflict and powerful emotions. 'Kids have always been willing to have books that faced up to tough things. For a long time adults wanted them to have nice books in which just the loveliest possible world was shown. I find kids like the exciting parts.'

Working with Children, Bernard Ashley

Our third author, Bernard Ashley, is the head teacher of a London primary school. In the following interview he talks about how he works alongside his pupils.

From time to time, I do a stint of four to six sessions with a class. Although I'm never the 'guest author' in my own school, I do this. I work with children. I give them all a notebook. It's not for me. It's for them. I tell them I don't want to see it. It's their camera. It's what they record things in, things that they think are interesting. I show them my own notebook and I tell them how I use it, and how I lay things out. One lovely example I heard on a bus going from Woolwich Ferry to East Ham town hall. We were going past a field that had been pre-fabs, and one woman turned to the other and said, *'I can remember these fields when they were all houses.'*

I show them the kind of pen I like to write with and how I use the notebook. I write on every other line and on every other page. What I try to emphasize is that it's just the means by which we get our thoughts down on paper. It has got to work for us, not us for it. And I show them some really messy pages to emphasize that ideas take precedence over any other consideration.

The other thing I do – which I know is obvious – is talk about basing their writing on *what they know*. We'll talk about things that have happened to us and maybe we'll decide to put two or three of them together.

I also introduce the de Bono thing. When you're stuck,

Finding your voice and finding a focus

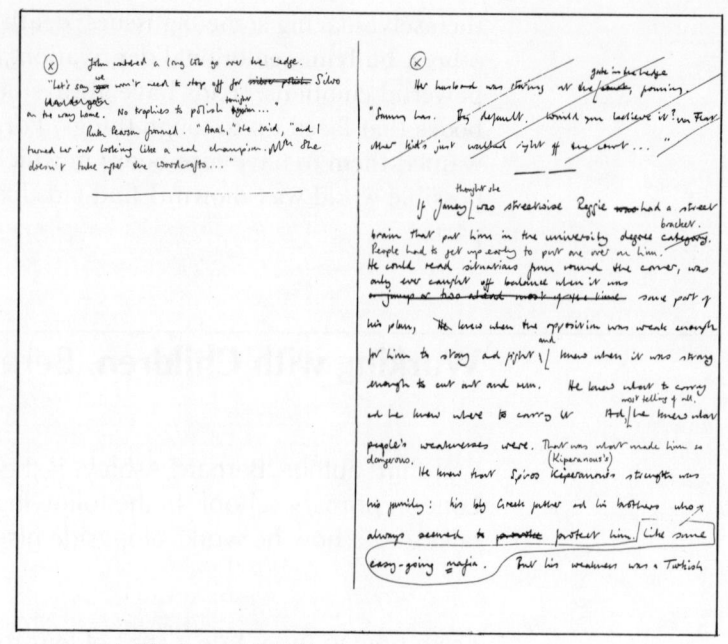

Bernard Ashley's notebook

look around you, and see what you can pick up from your surroundings. With one class I asked them to choose two objects in the room. They chose an inflatable globe and the radiator. Someone said, *'If you put the globe on top of the radiator it will get bigger.'* Someone else said, *'I could write a story about that, the world getting bigger and cracks appearing in the pavements.'*

Sometimes I like to do this thing out of Alec Clegg's book. We think about a person, someone we know. We think about the elements that go to make up that person's character, then we map those elements onto another character. We do things like taking the sorts of things a character typically says. For example, we can start with something like,

My grandfather always says, *'You can't help it if you can't do everything.'*

And if you can build this into a story, the whole thing comes to life.

A bit of a gimmick

It's a bit of a gimmick, but I do say when we're talking

about a story that what really is important is that you put down what you feel. I do ask them to put down what they feel, because that's really what's got to come through. Suppose they're writing about something that has happened to them, it's not enough to say '*I lost my dog*'. Because if they can remember how they felt and put it down in words, whoever reads what they have written will share that experience with them.

DRAMA

Johnny Salter, Aidan Chambers

Johnny Salter is a humorous play about finding your own voice when you belong to a family with class prejudiced views; to a gang which does not allow you to think for yourself and to a society which stereotypes the roles of boys and girls.

We have chosen two extracts; the first one introduces us to the gang.

A head comes up over the wall. It is CARROTS – *all tomboy and gawpy.*

CARROTS   Hallo, everybody!

They all look round and give a great moan.

CARROTS [*standing on the wall*]   Thanks for the friendly welcome, boys.

JOHNNY   Look, Carrots, go home. We don't want you. How often do we have to tell you?

CARROTS   I know. Sad isn't it! [*She offers a bag of sweets.*] Have a liquorice.

JOHNNY   Now that's different!

Yelling in glee, they crowd round her and snaffle liquorice. WRIGGLES *can't reach.* JOHNNY *hauls him on to the wall between him and* CARROTS.

JOHNNY   Come on, Wriggles.

CARROTS Well ... thanks for the vote of confidence, boys.

SPARKS Look, Carrots. We like you a lot. You know? It's nothing personal or anything. But we like your liquorice more. [*He takes one.*] May I? Thanks! But you know ... this is a boy's gang and ...

CARROTS Don't tell me ... I know [*jumping down*] girls is horrid. [*She sits on the dustbin.*]

SPARKS That's it. [*He gets his bike and straddles it alongside* CARROTS.]

CARROTS They are always on about clothes and boys and that sort of thing.

SPARKS That's it.

CARROTS They just moon about and giggle.

SPARKS That's it. You've got it. You understand fine.

CARROTS And you can't bear them.

SPARKS You know, for a girl you're quite intelligent. You're all there. Can't stick them. So ...

CARROTS So neither can I. Have another liquorice.

PUFF [*passing behind them and taking a liquorice as he goes*] Me too! My Mum says girls is easier to bring up than boys. My Mum says she wished she had half a dozen girls rather than me.

NYLON Knowing you, Puff, that doesn't surprise me!

CARROTS My Mum says just the opposite.

SPARKS [*wryly*] And that doesn't surprise me!

JOHNNY Parents are pretty hopeless anyhow. The only reason you have them is so they can embarrass you. Look at my Dad. He does nothing but go to work, garden, go to the local, and watch telly. Do you know, I don't think I've ever had a sensible conversation with my Dad!

PUFF That's just what I said about mine. Mine's just the same. It's not good enough. I think I'll start a Society for the Getting Rid of Parents.

NYLON [*sadly*] I ain't got a Dad.

SPARKS Then you're lucky, Nylon. Honest.

DRAMA: *Johnny Salter*, Aidan Chambers

WRIGGLES *has climbed the lamp-post as far as the ladder-bar. He is clinging on tightly.*

WRIGGLES   Johnny!

JOHNNY   Well, you're all right, Wriggles. Your Dad's all right.

WRIGGLES   I know ... It's not that ... It's ...

JOHNNY   Well, there you are. You've nothing to worry about.

WRIGGLES   It's not that. It's ...

JOHNNY   Well, what is it?

WRIGGLES   I'm stuck! I can't get down.

SPARKS   Oh, crikey, he's done it again. Come on, Johnny.

SPARKS *jumps off his bike and pushes it at* NYLON *who catches it and places it against the wall.* JOHNNY, SPARKS *and* PUFF *gather round the lamp-post.* CARROTS *watches from the dustbin.*

PUFF   How often have we told you ...

JOHNNY, SPARKS and PUFF   Don't climb things!

JOHNNY   You always get stuck.

WRIGGLES   I know. Get me down, Johnny.

JOHNNY   Come on. [*They build a human ladder up to* WRIGGLES. PUFF *is base, then* SPARKS, *then* JOHNNY.]

CARROTS   Be careful. If you drop him, he'll make a nasty hole in the pavement.

JOHNNY, SPARKS and NYLON [*in mock laughter*]   Ha! Ha! [*They get* WRIGGLES *down. Enter* MOGGS, *the Nightwatchman.*]

MOGGS   Now then, what's going on?

ALL   Moggs! Mr Moggs! Good old, Moggy, etc., *ad lib*. [*They crowd round* MOGGS. WRIGGLES *jumps up and hangs round his neck.*]

PUFF   Where you going, Mr Moggs? Can we come with you?

WRIGGLES   Yes. We'll come with you.

MOGGS   Steady, boys, steady. I'm not going anywhere, really. Just into town to do some shopping, like. Nothing much. Just to get a bit of baccy, and then back

up here to Joe's Place for me dinner, and me bait.
[MOGGS *puts* WRIGGLES *down and sits on the dustbin. They gather round.*]

SPARKS   Well, we can come. We'd help.

MOGGS   You – help! No fear! Not in town on Saturday morning.

JOHNNY   Then can we take the dog out?

MOGGS   You leave my Jessie alone. She had her pups last night.

General rejoicing.

JOHNNY   How many, Mr Moggs?

MOGGS   Four. Three bitches and a dog.

NYLON   Can I have one, Mr Moggs?

MOGGS   You can that, son, when they're weaned, so long as your Mum says yes.

NYLON   Then that stops that! Last time I asked for one she said she wouldn't have one in the place. They only messed on the carpet, she said.

They all commiserate.

MOGGS   What you all hanging about the streets for? Haven't you nothing to do?

JOHNNY   No, it's Saturday and it's boring.

PUFF   Saturday is horrid.

WRIGGLES   Don't like Saturday.

MOGGS   Why don't you have a game?

JOHNNY   Games are kids stuff!

SPARKS   We ain't kids any more.

MOGGS [*smiling*]   Oh. I see.

WRIGGLES   I dunno. I like games.

PUFF   But you're still a kid, Wriggles.

NYLON   Games ruffle up your clothes.

MOGGS   That so? Ah well. Must be off. [*He rises.*] Don't get up to any mischief, mind. Like last week when you tipped that dustbin all over that Barton boy.

JOHNNY   Over Bouncer? Well he deserved it.

SPARKS   Yes. He'd been asking for it all week. He's always bashing Wriggles or taking the mickey out of him.

JOHNNY   Yes. So we let him have it.

MOGGS   Ah well. Keep your noses clean. See you, boys!

All reply. Exit MOGGS. *They re-group round the lamp-post.* CARROTS *sits on the wall, alone.* WRIGGLES *sits on the dustbin and looks at a train-spotting book.*

SPARKS   I like old Moggy.

JOHNNY   Yes, so do I. It must be a funny job being a nightwatchman.

SPARKS   Yes. Scare-making a bit. All them cases in that dark factory.

PUFF   Works at Grimshaw's don't he?

NYLON   Yes.

PUFF   My Dad says he's past it. He says that if anyone burgled the place the old man probably wouldn't be able to do much about it.

SPARKS   Then your Dad's a nut. Even if he is a bit old, I bet Moggy would beat any burglar.

JOHNNY   Yea, so do I. And anyway old Grimshaw isn't no idiot. He wouldn't have a nightwatchman that couldn't look after all the valuable stuff there must be in that warehouse.

PUFF   My Dad says there must be thousands of pounds worth of stuff in that building.

SPARKS   And for once, Puff, your Dad's probably right.

CARROTS   [*pointing up the street with a look of horror*]   Oo, I say, you chaps, Look! GIRLS! Ugh!

CARROTS *dives behind the wall. The others yell in horror and follow her.* WRIGGLES *is left on the dustbin, bewildered at their sudden disappearance. As the girls enter he watches them with relish, waving coyly as they pass him.*

Enter THREE SCHOOLGIRLS. *Two are listening with 'gone' faces as the third tells her story. They sigh romantically from time to time.*

1ST. GIRL   Oh! It was terrific. I saw him at the Palladium. And we all screamed because he was so fab. He has eyes like great blue pools ... and long, gorgeous hair that shone in the lights. And he wore a suit with tight trousers and a polo-necked sweater.... And he sang this song about a girl he had lost. And it was called ... 'Fading Love'. [*The other two give great romantic sighs.*]

THE GIRLS *exit down the street. As they sigh, the gang's heads appear above the wall, all with horrified expressions on their faces and holding their noses as though they had just smelt a bad smell.*

ALL Poo! [*They climb on to the wall.*]

CARROTS Girls is horrid.

SPARKS Have you ever thought what it must be like to be a girl?

NYLON Crumbs, Sparks, please!

PUFF Cor, Sparks, shurrup – it's too awful on top of breakfast.

SPARKS No, but serious – have you? Drooling on like that about boys. [*He jumps down from the wall, takes up a mock-girl's stance and then imitates mockingly.*] OOO and he was fabulous ... You should have seen his eyes! Like mucky pools! And his hair ... OOO ... fab! Like tangled fuse wire! And he sang the most fab song called [*he jumps down and grabs* WRIGGLES *as though making love*] 'My Love for You is Like Mouldy Custard'.

They are all giggling.

WRIGGLES Hey but, Sparks, she didn't say that. She said ...

PUFF Gag him, Sparks!

They jump down and gather round WRIGGLES.

NYLON Poor Wriggles. You just don't understand.

PUFF But you will one day. When you is old as us and know about girls, you'll understand.

CARROTS Take a tip from me, Wriggles. Have nothing to do with them. I don't. Leave them strictly alone.

WRIGGLES But I like girls.

ALL What!

JOHNNY *and* SPARKS *grab* WRIGGLES *by the elbows and stand him on the dustbin.*

DRAMA: *Johnny Salter*, Aidan Chambers

JOHNNY [*scandalized*] But Wriggles, you can't. I mean, well, I mean. You just *can't*!

WRIGGLES Oh! Why?

SPARKS It's not allowed. It's high treason.

WRIGGLES Oh? What's that?

SPARKS Well – you know – like, it's against the gang.

JOHNNY Yes. It's against us.

PUFF Anyway, Wriggles, you ain't old enough to like girls.

NYLON No. You ain't old enough.

WRIGGLES How old do you have to be then?

CARROTS Honest, Wriggles! You're *never* old enough – leave them strictly alone.

PUFF Look, Carrots, shut up. What do you know about it? After all, you're only a girl.

JOHNNY [*being fatherly and adult*] You see, Wriggles, it's like this . . . Girls are not like boys. Well . . . you know . . . Girls is girls and boys is boys.

WRIGGLES I know, Johnny. That's why I like girls.

JOHNNY But, Wriggles, you can't. Well, look. You see . . . Oh, crumbs! Hasn't your Dad told you anything yet?

WRIGGLES Anything about what?

JOHNNY About girls.

WRIGGLES Dunno . . . Nothing what I can remember.

SPARKS Well, has he talked to you about . . . well about the birds and the bees?

WRIGGLES No, don't think so. [*Pause.*] Oh yes he did!

ALL [*very eager and crowding round*] Did he? What did he say?

WRIGGLES He said that if I didn't keep away from that bloody bee it would sting me.

Reading and talking

■ Read through the extract. Then talk about:
 – each of the characters and their relationship with each other;
 – the humour in the situation and dialogue;

59

- the attitudes of the individual members of the gang towards parents and girls;
- the image of girls as presented by the three schoolgirls.

■ This play was written a long time ago. How far do you think young people's attitudes have changed?

The second extract introduces one of the families:

Act 2

The garden of the GRIMSHAWS', *local factory owners. A warm sunny afternoon the same Saturday. A wall; suggestion of trees, flowers and grass. A garden table and four chairs; a small garden bench by the wall; and two deckchairs. In one sits* MR GRIMSHAW, *asleep under a newspaper. In the other sits* MRS GRIMSHAW, *knitting.*

A bird is whistling almost cheekily. MR GRIMSHAW *stirs, takes up the paper and begins to read it. We have not yet seen his face. When we do, he appears, well-built middle aged, bald, and very bad-tempered of face. He is a wealthy factory owner who has 'come up the hard way'.* MRS GRIMSHAW *is also middle-aged, but is a far more 'comfortable' and sympathetic person than her husband, by whom she refuses to be bullied.*

MR GRIMSHAW   It's no good, y'know.

MRS GRIMSHAW   No, dear.

MR GRIMSHAW   We haven't been the same since the war.

MRS GRIMSHAW   No, dear.

MR GRIMSHAW   Ruined! The country's ruined!

MRS GRIMSHAW   Yes, dear.

SALLY [*off*]   The red dress isn't pressed, Mum.

MRS GRIMSHAW   Then try the pink one, dear.

SALLY [*off*]   But I don't like the pink one. Can't I wear my tennis shorts and a shirt?

MRS GRIMSHAW   Not today, dear. Colonel Chunter is coming to tea and you know how old-fashioned the Chunters are.

SALLY [*Off*]   But Mum ...

DRAMA: *Johnny Salter*, Aidan Chambers

MRS GRIMSAHW   Now do as you're told, dear.

SALLY [*Off*[But Mum ...

MR GRIMSHAW [*irritably dropping the newspaper to his knees, and bellowing in the direction of* SALLY]   Do as your Mother says, confound you, girl!
Pause.
She's getting as bad as the rest of her age. Contradictory. Always wanting to do different from what they're told. Look at this long-haired specimen here. Looks like an overgrown teddy-bear.
[*Shows* MRS GRIMSHAW *the paper.*]

MRS GRIMSHAW   That's Prince Charles, dear.

MR GRIMSHAW   Is it? Oh yes, so it is. Well that's what I say. All the same. Good for nothing but hitting old women on the head and lounging about the place.

MRS GRIMSHAW   Who is, dear? Prince Charles?

MR GRIMSHAW   No. Teenagers. Teenagers today. Now in my day, you had to do as you were told, and sharp, or you were given a good beating. And that was that. Thank goodness I wasn't brought up in this modern namby-pamby way. Didn't do me a bit of harm either. I'm perfectly normal. Not twisted in any way. Am I?

MRS GRIMSHAW   No, dear.

MR GRIMSHAW   Well ... there you are then.
Pause.

MRS GRIMSHAW   I do wish the Chunters weren't coming to tea today. One's never quite sure about Sally's boy friends, and I've never even heard of this one.

MR GRIMSHAW   Confound it! Don't say Sally's bringing a boy friend here today!

MRS GRIMSHAW   But of course, dear. Why do you think she's so concerned about her dress? She's been talking about it since she came in for lunch.

MR GRIMSHAW   Good heavens, Milly, you don't mean we've got to put up with one of these long-haired morons half this afternoon and for tea, do you?

MRS GRIMSHAW   He may be neither long-haired nor moronic, dear. I just said I'd prefer to find out without the Chunters being here.

MR GRIMSHAW   And if she's picked him up in that café place you were soft enough to let her work in, then I suppose he'll be an out-of-work yodeller from a lemonade group.

MRS GRIMSHAW   They're called 'pop' groups, dear, and as he's only fourteen and still at school, you can hardly call him out of work.

MR GRIMSHAW   He's certainly not in work if he's still at school. They do nothing at school these days. One long holiday. Don't know what these teachers are thinking about. All we turn out now is half-baked oafs who can't spell their own names.

Enter SALLY.

SALLY   Will this do, Mum? It feels awful.

MRS GRIMSHAW   It's lovely, Sally. Very nice. Isn't it, dear?

MR GRIMSHAW   What? Oh, yes. And while you're here, missy, before you go off and change to meet this boy of yours, tell us something about him.

SALLY [*she sits at a seat by the garden table*]   I already have.

A door bell rings.

SALLY [*off*]   That'll be Johnny, Mum. I'll go.

MRS GRIMSHAW   Now remember, Herbert. Give him a chance.

MR GRIMSHAW   If he's a savage I shall give him a club!

Enter SALLY *and* JOHNNY. JOHNNY *is very nervous and watches* SALLY *carefully for directions as to what to do and say. He makes a brave effort to be polite and correct.*

SALLY   Daddy, this is Johnny Salter.

JOHNNY   Hello, sir. It's kind of you to allow me to come to tea.

GRIMSHAW *looks him up and down contemptuously.*

MR GRIMSHAW   Oh. Hello, young man. Ah! Yes, not at all. [*Returning to his paper in disgust.*] Delighted.

MRS GRIMSHAW   I'm Mrs Grimshaw, Johnny. Sally's Mother. How-do-you-do?

JOHNNY   Very well, thank you, Mrs Grimshaw.

MRS GRIMSHAW [*to* MR GRIMSHAW]   Would you like your club, dear?

DRAMA: *Johnny Salter*, Aidan Chambers

MR GRIMSHAW Eh?

MRS GRIMSHAW Sit down, Johnny. [*Indicates seat.*]

JOHNNY Thanks.

MR GRIMSHAW [*reluctantly doing what he considers his duty*] Sally tells me you want to take her to a youth club tonight.

JOHNNY Yes, sir. If you'll let me.

MR GRIMSHAW Don't know that I agree with youth clubs. Dens of vice most of 'em. Breeding grounds for gang warfare.

SALLY *is making elaborate signs, from behind her father's chair, to* JOHNNY *to keep quiet.*

MRS GRIMSHAW Perhaps. but I wouldn't say that Johnny looked much of a savage. Would you, dear?

MR GRIMSHAW *grunts and goes back to his paper.*

MRS GRIMSHAW We're expecting visitors, Johnny. When they come we'll have tea.

JOHNNY *starts up, taken aback.*

JOHNNY Visitors ... I ...

SALLY [*pushing him down*] It's all right. Only the Chunters. They're quite harmless really.

Door bell rings.

MRS GRIMSHAW That'll be them. I'll go.

Exit MRS GRIMSHAW.

JOHNNY [*loud whisper*] What'll I do? Who are they?

SALLY Just say yes and no in the right places.

Talking and reading

- Talk about the members of the Grimshaw family and their relationships with each other.
- When you read the extract a second time, experiment with different kinds of voices, so as to bring out the background, attitudes and differences of the four characters in this scene. Don't fall into the trap of thinking that rich, middle-aged people all speak with 'posh' accents and that Johnny Salter, who lives 'on the other side of town', speaks 'common'!

- What difficulties do you think Sally experiences growing up in her family? What evidence is there that she is finding her own 'voice'?

Within each scene of a play, just as within each chapter of a novel, the writer might wish to focus the reader's attention on a particular character, attitude, event, time or tension in the play.

Talking and reading

- What do you think Aidan Chambers hopes that producers of his play will focus on in these two scenes?
- Read both the playwright's stage directions which precede the entrance of the Chunter family and the opening dialogue.

There are loud greetings off. The loudest comes from a domineering woman. A second later, enter MRS CHUNTER *followed by* COL. CHUNTER *and* PENELOPE, *their daughter. All three are ridiculous caricatures of real people.* MRS CHUNTER *is a modern Victorian aunt: She holds herself in and straight, allowing only the occasional grandiose gesture to emphasize what she says. She barks at both her husband and her daughter, bullying them with every word. To other people she gives huge and meaningless smiles. She is patronizing and always 'correct'.* COL. CHUNTER *is older. He carries a walking-stick and his head nods constantly. It has become a reflex with him to agree with his wife. His speech can only be described as 'strangled'.* PENELOPE *is dressed in riding clothes and carries a crop. She simpers and giggles all the time, and her hands and feet suggest that she suffers paroxysms which probably result from the brow-beating her mother indulges in when she speaks to her daughter.* MRS CHUNTER *sweeps across the stage, greeting* SALLY *as she does so. Her family follow in her wake, like dutiful dogs.* MRS GRIMSHAW *watches it all, mildly amused, from the garden table.*

MRS CHUNTER   ... and there's Sally. Hello, my dear. How charming you look; so fresh. Isn't she, Hector?

COL. CHUNTER   Stunning, dear. Reminds me of ...

MRS CHUNTER   And who is this mannikin? A new playmate? Isn't he handsome, Hector?

FINDING A FOCUS: *A Dead Pig and My Father*, Nina Bawden

COL. CHUNTER Handsome ...

MRS CHUNTER And what is the dear mannikin's name, Sally?

SALLY Johnny Salter. This is Mrs Chunter, Johnny.

MRS CHUNTER Hello, Johnny. Let me introduce you to my daughter, Penelope. I'm sure you'll get on splendidly. Won't they, Hector?

Writing Continue the dialogue. Remember to:
- include all the people who are present in this scene;
- give stage directions which help the actors to be occupied when they are not speaking;
- decide *before* you start to write what the *focus* of your scene is to be.

Drama Try out your finished scenes. How successful have you been in keeping continuity in characterisation, and in developing your new characters?

FINDING A FOCUS

A Dead Pig and My Father, Nina Bawden

As readers we learn to become skilled at detecting what it is that the writer wishes to draw our attention to, whether it be a place, situation, atmosphere, a character's viewpoint or the writer's own sympathies. The writer Nina Bawden describes the most important thing in her 'picture' when she recalls a vivid childhood memory:

One of my earliest memories is standing in Tilbury Docks, near London, looking at a dead pig in the water. It was floating belly upwards, a tight yellowish balloon, veined with blue. It was surrounded by several planks of wood that were being pushed into the side by a passenger liner that was coming into dock. When these planks crowded together and bumped the swollen-bellied pig, it bobbed in the water and squeaked.

Finding your voice and finding a focus

I was four years old. I know how old I was because my mother was standing beside me, holding my baby brother. He was wrapped in a shawl and he had a face like a wet, wrinkled prune. He was two months old and he had been born just after my fourth birthday.

We were standing on the dockside, my mother and my baby brother and me, because my father's ship was coming in. He was a marine engineer, coming home from Australia after a long time away and he hadn't seen my baby brother so this was an important occasion. My mother said, 'Look at the big ship, Nina. See if you can see Daddy.'

But I was more interested in the dead pig. I went on watching it as it bobbed and squeaked in the water.

Children don't always feel what adults expect them to feel, nor see what adults expect them to see.

Drawing and writing

Draw or describe two pictures based on Nina Bawden's experience. One of your pictures should focus on the mother and show what she is seeing and feeling; the other on Nina should show what she is seeing and feeling.

Going Back, Penelope Lively

Often in a long novel a writer will draw on a particularly sharp memory to provide a focus within a chapter. One such powerful incident is described by Penelope Lively in this extract from *Going Back*.

The quarry was a green cup in the fields. Bramble and hawthorn humped down its sides into the green grassy bottom. Standing on the bank at the top of the hill we looked down into it, and beyond to the spinney and beyond that again into distances that became blue instead of green, away and away to the brown rim of Exmoor against the sky. And the warblers in the quarry competed with the chaffinches in the spinney: the whole green and growing place fluttered and sang. 'Orchids,' we said, remembering. And we abandoned Betty's basket behind the hedge and ran, slipping and skidding, down into the quarry.

The orchids grew always in one place, at the far end, in a little cul-de-sac between high cliffs of bramble. Early purple orchids, in banks, and rare green ones that we did not know the name of, and, later, bee orchids. The early purples would be out now, and there were lots, not rare and special, so we could pick some for Betty.

We whooped and dodged between the mountainous brambles. All ahead and all around there was pink bramble blossom and foaming white may. Somewhere behind and out of sight we could hear Mike whistling: he whistled something complicated that we had heard him play on the violin and up above on the as yet bare branches of an ash a blackbird lurched down and whistled back at him, a simpler version. Edward bounded ahead to the orchid place and I followed. He went round a corner and I lost him.

'Edward ... *Edward*!'

He didn't answer. When I came up to him he was all among the orchids, staring at something, gone silent.

It was a rabbit's head, lying between pinnacles of orchid where bees unconcernedly clung and fed. It had empty eye sockets but shreds of fur stuck to it still, and the rag of an ear. It was hideous, appalling. We stared at it in revulsion, unable to tear ourselves away.

And then we heard Mike, scrambling among the bushes, and we turned and fled back to him, through the bramble and hawthorn that had darkened suddenly and become canyons, huge gloomy places from which we wanted to get away.

'Where are these orchids of yours, then?' said Mike amiably.

And Edward said, 'There aren't any. We've got to go back now.' And pelted away up to the lane with Mike following, not knowing what had happened. The quarry was blasted for us now by what it held. We were ashamed of it, as though it were our fault. We didn't want Mike to know, not ever.

The rabbit's head became my private symbol of horror. For years it haunted my dreams. Now, it comes back to

Finding your voice and finding a focus

me in other forms: a newspaper photograph of distant wars, a crumpled car beside a motorway.

And we never went into the quarry again.

Reading, talking and writing

- Read the passage aloud or quietly to yourselves. From whose viewpoint is the memory recalled?
- Notice and jot down how the writer:
  - selects details to build up an impression and the mood of a perfect spring day;
  - achieves a contrast between the mood at the beginning of the incident and the finding of the rabbit's head, e.g. use of colour;
  - uses very little dialogue. Why do you think she introduces it at certain points in the passage?
  - uses the adult, Mike, to emphasise the children's horror at what they have seen;
  - has *shaped* this memory into a compact and spare piece of descriptive writing of about 500 words.
- Does Penelope Lively's account remind you of any occasion when a place you knew well was suddenly changed (it could be a change for the better) because of an incident that took place there?
- Look at all the rough notes you have made and re-read the extract. Write a short descriptive piece of writing in which you:
  - set the scene, establish the time of day or season of the year, mood and atmosphere;
  - find an effective way of introducing and focusing on an incident, a 'find' or another person which changes the whole situation;
  - think carefully about your final sentence.
- Share your writing with a friend. Write down, in pencil, comments and suggestions which, in your opinion, would make the piece of writing more effective for future readers. Be prepared to make any changes you think necessary before finally presenting your work to your teacher.

The following short piece of prose and two poems illustrate the ways in which the three writers have focused on different aspects of the same subject – Wind.

Wind, Edward Storey

The autumn so far is very uncertain and its days are unpredictable. Conditions change overnight. Even hours are different seasons. One day is calm and filled with sunlight. The next day can be dull and wintry with strong winds.

Today has been a day when the winds have reached gale force. Trees have been ripped out of the ground. Fences have been blown down. Gates swing open on broken hinges and the streets are littered with roof-tiles and garden debris. Apples that were ready for picking and waiting for labourers have now been shaken out of the trees. The orchards are full of bruises.

Low black clouds are still being buffeted about the sky like boats in harbour. They bump and groan, spilling great splashes of rain that whip the ground and scratch the window panes.

Drivers have been warned not to drive too fast or travel on exposed roads. How would I get to Spalding today, I wonder, or Ramsey or Chatteris. I know that in this weather I would be afraid to drive along Deeping High Bank or Ramsey Forty Foot. On that particular tightrope of a road you would be lucky to keep your balance in a ten-ton tank. A car would be blown off the road and into the drain or fields in seconds – a considerable drop whichever way you went.

We can combat snow and rain. We can control floods. We can put out fires. But we sit helplessly listening to the wind straining at the windows to get in, thundering down the chimney, slamming doors and making walls tremble. Nothing in this landscape makes a man feel so defeated. In the spring a farmer must stand by utterly helpless and watch his seeds torn out of the ground and blown away in one of the dust storms I've spoken of before. In winter he can keep a close eye on the fresh water coming into the fens from the uplands and wait anxiously for each high tide. He can control the flow of water through the sluices and into the rivers. But when the wind blows as it blows today these fears are multiplied. You cannot build sea-walls or sluice-gates against the wind. It attacks across the whole breadth of the land. It is the invisible enemy.

Workings of the Wind, James Berry

Wind doesn't always topple trees
and shake houses to pieces.

Wind plays
all over woods, with weighty ghosts
in swings in thousands,
swinging from every branch.

Wind doesn't always rattle windows
and push, push at walls.

Wind whistles
down cul-de-sacs and worries
dry leaves and old newspapers to leap
and curl like kite tails.

Wind doesn't always dry out
sweaty shirts and blouses.

Wind scatters
pollen dust of flowers, washes
people's and animals' faces
and combs out birds' feathers.

Wind doesn't always whip up waves
into white horses.

Wind shakes up
tree-shadows to dance on rivers,
to jig about on grass, and hanging
lantern light to play signalman.

Wind doesn't always run wild
kicking tinny dustbin lids.

Wind makes
leafy limbs bow to red roses
and bob up and down outside windows
and makes desk papers fly up indoors.

A Windy Day, Andrew Young

This wind brings all dead things to life,
Branches that lash the air like whips
And dead leaves rolling in a hurry
Or peering in a rabbits' bury
Or trying to push down a tree;
Gates that fly open to the wind
And close again behind,
And fields that are a flowing sea
And make the cattle look like ships;
Straws glistening and stiff
Lying on air as on a shelf,
And pond that leaps to leave itself;
And feathers too that rise and float,
Each feather changed into a bird,
And line-hung sheets that crack and strain;
Even the sun-greened coat,
That through so many winds has served,
The scarecrow struggles to put on again.

Reading and talking

Read through the prose extract and the two poems in order to enjoy the sounds, movements and pictures expressed in each.

Writing and reading

- On a second reading, this time aloud, listen for:
  - the words and phrases which focus on *sounds*;
  - the words which suggest *movement*;
  - the *images*;
  - *key* phrases.
- On the next page we have given you an example of one method of recording your findings. Add your own words and phrases to the columns already begun.

Finding your voice and finding a focus

FOCUS	*A Windy Day*	*Workings of the Wind*	*Wind*
SOUND	lash fields/flowing glistening/stiff leaps/leave feathers/float	**Doesn't:** topple trees .... **Does:** wind/ woods/weighty	black/buffeted boats bump
MOVEMENT	lash rolling peering push fly	**Doesn't:** topple shake .... **Does:** plays	ripped/blown
IMAGES (pictures)	branches like whips dead leaves caught in rabbits' holes fields of grass rippling	**Doesn't:** .... **Does:** leaves and newspapers twirling through air	Vehicles being blown off high banked road into field or fen-land drain below
KEY PHRASES	?	?	It is the invisible enemy

- When you have completed your columns, talk about each writer's approach to the subject and the effectiveness of the writing.

Focusing on the sharing and presentation of one of the poems will involve you in making certain decisions as well as helping you to become more confident as readers of poetry — readers with your 'ears' as well as your 'eyes'.

Dramatic presentation

Choose one of the poems to present as a group to the rest of the class.

To help with your preparation, read pages 186–7 (in 'Focus on Dialogue in Poems'). You will need to decide:
- how to use effectively the natural voices of the people in your group;
- which lines should be spoken by solo voices, which by two or three voices and which by the whole group;

- how to achieve change of *pace* and *volume* in order to bring out the *sound, movement* and *images* in the poems;
- on the standing positions of your group when you present your poem.

Work sharing Share your work. Comment upon different interpretations and their effectiveness. Talk about what you have learned from preparing for this presentation.

Edward Storey believes 'that landscapes are important to a writer, whether he is a nature poet or a novelist, a prose writer or a dramatist. He takes from it his images, his scenes, even the speech rhythms he uses. We are all products of some kind of landscape. Our geographical environment influences us as much as our social environment.'

Writing Choose one of the four elements or an aspect of weather. Write a description in which you focus on the idea that your chosen subject is an *enemy*. But before you choose, think about the landscape in which you live:
- Is it an area of low rainfall but high winds as in the Fens where Edward Storey lives?
- Do you experience heavy snowfalls in winter so that lambs have to be rescued?
- You might live in an inner city area occasionally attacked by dense fog.

Talking
- Share your writing and talk about how you think the environment round you has influenced your life.
- Do you agree with Edward Storey that physical surroundings influence us as much as the people around us?

3 Shifting viewpoints

PICTURE BOOKS

If At First You Do Not See, Ruth Brown

Mmm ... lovely, cold ice-cream.

... or is it?
If you look at this picture from another viewpoint it won't make your mouth water but it might make you smile.

Some of the best writers and illustrators of picture books help us to appreciate that there is always more than one way of 'seeing' a person or a situation.

One writer and illustrator who does this with understanding and humour is John Burningham.

PICTURE BOOKS: *Come Away From the Water, Shirley*, John Burningham

Come Away from the Water, Shirley, John Burningham

Of course it's far too cold for swimming, Shirley

This is the first page of a picture book by John Burningham.

Talking

- How do you think each person in the picture is hoping to spend the day on the beach?
- At this point in the story we cannot be sure whose viewpoint is being expressed in the words 'Of course it's far too cold for swimming, Shirley'.
  Take each character in turn and say the words in such a way as to show who is speaking and the attitude

Shifting viewpoints

of the speaker, e.g. assume the man is speaking. How might he say the words if he were:
- speaking to the child;
- speaking to the woman;
- reluctant to go swimming;
- disappointed that he couldn't go swimming;
- in a bad temper?

We now pick up the story on the fourth double-page 'opening'.

Don't stroke that dog, Shirley, you don't know where he's been

PICTURE BOOKS: *Come Away From the Water, Shirley*, John Burningham

Talking

- Have you had to change your mind about anything, e.g. the dog?
- Has the identity of the speaker become clearer?
- Were your predictions correct about how each person hoped to spend time on the beach?
- What is happening to Shirley?

Shifting viewpoints

Look at the eighth double-page 'opening':

> # Your father might have a game with you when he's had a little rest

It now becomes clear who is speaking to Shirley, but there is also another voice, that of the author expressing *his viewpoint*.

Talking

- How does he show how far apart the parents' 'real' world is from Shirley's 'imaginary' one?
- From all the extracts we have chosen, what comment is John Burningham making about the family and their relationships with each other?
- Where do you think his sympathies lie?

PICTURE BOOKS: *Come Away From the Water, Shirley,* John Burningham

Writing and drawing

John Burningham tells his story in two single-page pictures (one at the beginning and one at the end) and ten double-page 'openings'.

- If you are not familiar with the story, use the extracts in their correct order to create your own version. Keep to the same number of pages as in the original but use your own style of illustration.

    Give your story a title.

    When your stories are completed, read *Come Away from the Water, Shirley* and compare it with yours.

- If you already know this story, use the same idea to present another situation in which different viewpoints are being expressed. One double-page opening might say it all!

    Think of a suitable title.

CHARACTERS IN FICTION
The Best Day of My Easter Holidays, Jane Gardam

Our first impressions of people are often influenced by:
- their appearance and manner of speaking;
- what we know about their past;
- their behaviour towards us;
- their attitudes towards other people;
- what other people have to say about them, but most of all by;
- the kinds of people we are and how we 'see' ourselves.

When we get to know people better, it is likely that we change our views of them as we discover more about them, more about ourselves and our relationship with them.

It is just the same with people in books. As *readers*, we must be prepared to shift our viewpoint as the characters are developed and the story unfolds.

In the following extract from a short story by Jane Gardam, we are introduced to Jolly Jackson by Ned Egerton and, like him, we form our first impressions.

The best day of my Easter holidays was the day we met Jolly Jackson. This year we went to Jamaica for our holidays because my father was working there and so we spent all his fees although it was still expensive and we didn't get any rake-off. When I told all the American people in our hotel we were there on my father's fees they thought it was very funny and said things to my father like 'I hear you're travelling light, bud,' and slapped him over the back in a way that puzzled him and made him angry.

The people in our hotel were all very, very rich. One was so rich he got paralysed, the beach-boy told me. Like Midas one side of him got turned to gold. He dribbled. The only one not rich was a vicar. He had gone there to a conference. My mother met him in the sea and they talked up to their knees. 'How lucky we are,' said the vicar in a HUGE American accent, 'in this so glorious country, enjoying the gifts of God. It is Eden itself.' Then he shouted 'FLAMING HADES' and fell flat on his stomach in the sea because he had been stung by a sea-egg. 'Help, help,' called my mother and everyone came running off the beach and dragged the vicar up the sand – blood everywhere. 'Ammonia!' cried someone. 'Only thing for a sea-egg is to pee on it,' said the beach-raker. 'Git gone,' said the beach-boy and my mother said, 'Come along now Ned dear, it's time we set off for Duns River Falls.' The other women turned away, too and only the men were left standing around the vicar who had five black spikes sticking out of his foot and was rolling about in agony. 'They never do no permanent harm, ma'am,' said the beach-boy to my mother, 'just pain and anguish for a day,' and he was laughing like anything – well, like a Jamaican and they laugh a great deal. I don't know if they did try peeing on the vicar or if they did if it was one or all of them. I kept thinking of the whole crowd standing round and peeing on the vicar and I laughed like a Jamaican all the way to Duns River Falls until my parents said, 'Shut up or there'll be trouble.'

Duns River Falls are some waterfalls that drop into the sea. I had expected them about as high as a tower but they were only about as high as my father. Also they had built a road over them and kiosks, etc., and ticket offices and I was fed up because I had wanted to stay on the beach.

My mother said, 'Well, now we're here –' and we began to park the car when a huge man came dancing along the road in pink and blue clothes and a straw hat and opened the door and shook hands with my father. 'Hullo Daddy,' he shouted, 'an' how are you today?' (Everyone starts 'An' how are you today.') 'Now then Daddy, outs you get and in the back. I gonna sit with Mummy.'

Now my father is a man who is very important at home and nobody tells him what to do. In Jamaica he doesn't wear his black suit and stiff collar or his gold half-glasses, but even in an orange shirt and a straw hat you can tell he is very important. Oh yes man. But when this great big man told him to get out and sit in the back he got out and sat in the back, and my mother's eyes went large and wide. 'Stop for nobody and dat's advice,' they had said in our hotel, 'Jamaica is a very inflammatory place. Yes sir.' Well this man held out the biggest hand I've ever seen, pink on the front, and said, 'My name's Jolly Jackson and what's yours?'

My father said, 'Hum. Hum. Ahem,' but my mother said, 'Mrs Egerton,' and held out her hand and I sprang up and down and said, 'My name's Ned, man,' and my father said, 'That will do.'

'This boy talks Jamaican, yes sir,' said Jolly Jackson, 'and now I gonna take you to see the wonderful Public Gardens followed by a tour of the surrounding countryside where you will find growing, pineapples, coffee beans, tea, avocado, coconuts and every single thing. Every fruit in all the world grow in Jamaica. Jamaica is the best country in the world and the sun is always shining.'

At that moment it began to rain in the most tremendous torrents and as our car was going up a hill which was probably once part of the waterfall and going about the same sort of angle, great waves began to come rushing down on us and the car spluttered and stopped and then turned sideways and began to be washed away.

'This is one of the famous Jamaican rainstorms,' said Jolly Jackson. 'The rain in Jamaica is the best in the world. It is very necessary rain. It rushes over the ground and disappears into the sea. In a minute it will be gone.'

We sat there for about half an hour and the rain hit the road like ten million bullets and went up from it in steam and the trees above dripped it back. Waves washed round our sideways wheels and my mother said, 'What happens if a car comes the other way?'

'Don't worry,' said Jolly Jackson, 'everything stop in a Jamaica rainstorm,' and then a huge great petrol tanker with all its lights on came tearing round the corner and down the hill towards us, screeched its brakes and skidded into the side of the road and fell into a ditch.

'Here comes the sun now,' said Jolly Jackson in a hasty voice, 'away we go,' and he got the car going and turned up the hill again and off before the driver of the petrol tanker had got the door open and got a look at us.

He was right and the sun came out and everything shone and steamed. When we got to the Public Gardens Jolly Jackson put his foot on the accelerator and roared

CHARACTERS IN FICTION: *The Best Day of My Easter Holidays*, Jane Gardam

through, past the ticket office. He was out and had all of us out in about a quarter of a second and all of us off down a path before my mother could even mop up her face.

'This here is the famous Jamaica red tree,' he said. 'This here is oleander, that there is the ban-yan tree only fifty year old, big as a mountain. That there is a waterfall. Now this boy and Mummy are gonna stand in the waterfall and have a photo.' He took the camera from round my father's neck, undid it and went click, click. Sometimes he turned the camera towards himself and went click, click and my father said, 'I say, look here –'

'Now,' he said, 'you will take a photograph of me,' and he stood inside a very dark trellis tunnel full of great big pale green lilies like long bells hanging, and stretched up and smelled one, arching his very long back, and a big white smile on his face. He stood there for a very long time even though my mother said 'It's in the dark.' In the end she said, 'Oh well,' and went click and then Jolly Jackson moved on.

I've never seen my parents go so fast. He simply ran up and down paths, in and out of groves and places, pointing things out, picking things – sometimes great huge branches of things. 'Take it, take it. Plenty more. Jamaica can grow everything.' Once he stopped dead and we all crashed into his back. He gathered us all together and said, 'Look now, just there. That is the true Jamaica humming bird,' and there of course was a humming bird with its lovely curly tail. It was sipping from a rosy flower. There are thousands of them at our hotel all round our table at lunch every single day. We didn't even notice them much after the first week, but now we all said 'Ooooooooooh.' Jolly Jackson somehow made you say 'Ooooooooooh.' Yes man.

*

We seemed somehow after a very long time to get back to the same place, I don't know how. But it was terribly hot in the car and we didn't have any idea where we were. Then we saw the petrol tanker in the ditch and crowds and crowds trying to get it out and everybody smiling. Jolly Jackson's police friends were there and a lot of his other friends and we all got out again to shake hands, and we bought a pineapple for one dollar thirty which made my mother say, 'Fortnum and Mason!' Jolly Jackson introduced us to hundreds of his friends. Afterwards we went back towards the Falls again and we nearly hit another car and the driver leaned out and shouted a lot of queer language at us ending in Jackson. 'Is he your friend, too?' my mother asked, and Jolly Jackson said, 'No, I know him but he is not my friend.'

'Now, we all go in the Falls,' he said when we got to the parking place. 'All take off your clothes and we walk up the Falls, five hundred feet of pure Jamaican waterfall. Perfectly safe. Nobody never falls in, never.'

'NO,' said my father and gave him six dollars.

'Seven,' said Jolly Jackson, and my father gave him seven dollars, and we went off to look at the Falls by ourselves, my mother saying things like, 'Quite ridiculous. You are an utter fool, James. Daylight robbery,' and my father saying it was worth it just to be still alive.

Somehow going up the Falls was very dull though, without Jolly Jackson and we didn't stay long. Everyone looked very white and ugly and touristy and quiet. My mother even said as we left, and went to the car again, 'I suppose seven dollars was *enough*, James? He really did us rather well I suppose. We did *see* a lot. It took two hours.' But my father said 'Pah! Enough! Look!' and we saw Jolly Jackson by the car park all alone and dancing in the road.

I said I wanted to go and say goodbye to him again but they said, no. I said it wouldn't take long but they said, no dear, come along. 'Come along,' they said. 'Let's go back to the beach, let's see what's happened to the poor old vicar.' But that – the silly vicar and the man all paralysed with gold – didn't interest me any more. All that interested me was Jolly Jackson and I watched him and watched him, so beautiful, out of the back window of the car, getting smaller and smaller. And he waved and waved to me as he danced and danced. He danced and danced not moving his feet but with all his body and his lovely smiling face. He was dancing and dancing and dancing and dancing in the very middle of the big main road.

That was the best day of my Easter holidays.

(B – Egerton. Rubbish. See me.)

CHARACTERS IN FICTION: *The Best Day of My Easter Holidays*, Jane Gardam

Talking

- In the story we are seeing everyone from young Ned's point of view. Is there anything that he would not fully understand or be sympathetic to in the situation?
- What do we learn about Ned's family background? Why do you think he finds Jolly Jackson such an appealing character?

Drama

- Work in pairs. One of you take on the character of Ned Egerton, Mrs Egerton, Mr Egerton, or Jolly Jackson. The other partner is a friend.

   In conversation, recall some of the events of the day on which 'you' met Jolly Jackson or Jolly Jackson met the Egertons. For example, you might choose to become Mrs Egerton talking to a writer friend about her meeting with the vicar in the sea. The 'friend' should also develop the conversation by asking questions and commenting on the behaviour described.

- In small groups, improvise a scene in which the Egerton family are back in England. Some friends have been invited to hear about their holiday and see the photographs.

   Remember that time has passed and it is likely that the family may view the events of that day and Jolly Jackson differently now.

   Will Ned remember, with amusement, the embarrassment of his parents? How will he describe the situations being talked about or shown in the photographs?

   As the scene develops, choose one 'photograph' on which to focus everyone's attention. Through the use of the 'flashback' technique, your group (or another group in the class) could recreate the image in the photograph.

Writing

Mrs Egerton is a writer. Assume that she keeps a writer's notebook in which she records memorable events and scraps of conversation which she might, at some time, use in her stories.

- Write down the jottings she might have made about that day in the Easter holidays.
- Script one of your pieces of improvisation. Give it to another pair or group to try out and then be prepared to

85

Talking

redraft parts of it that don't seem to work out as you had hoped.

As writers we always have to make a choice about whether to write in the first or third person. When a writer refers to herself as 'I', we say that she is writing in the first person. In this story, Jane Gardam writes from the viewpoint of Ned.

What are the advantages for the writer in adopting a first person viewpoint in this story?

It might come as a surprise to get to the end of the story and realise that the author intends us to read this as an essay written by Ned for his teacher.

- Does Jane Gardam convince you?
- How far do you agree with the grade given and the comment?
- What do you think the teacher would have said to Egerton when they met to discuss the writing?
- How would Ned have defended his essay?

One of the most important shifts in viewpoint we have to make during and after completing a piece of writing is to look at it from a *reader's* point of view. Sharing your writing in its early stages with friends, as well as your teacher, should help you to decide where you need to make changes and so avoid ever having the comment 'Rubbish. See Me.' on any of your work!

In class discussion you must have been told many times to 'keep an open mind' and 'listen to other people's points of view' as well as expressing your own.

When we feel very strongly about a particular issue, this advice is difficult to follow. However, if we want to develop as *thinkers* we must not close our minds to the fact that we might wish to revise our first opinions. It is exciting to be able to change one's point of view after discussion and consideration.

Brainstorming

Work in groups. You will need two large sheets of paper and a pencil. Ask one person to jot down all the ideas in any order.

Remember as a group:
- Accept all ideas; the more the better.

CHARACTERS IN FICTION: *On the Edge*, Gillian Cross

- Do not criticise anyone's suggestions; listen to each new idea and build on it.
- Keep an open mind about the subject under discussion.

Now, do a Brainstorming exercise on:

> The family

Give yourselves time to *think* as well as to speak; it is not a race to see which group can finish first!

On the second sheet of paper group your ideas under headings, e.g.

> Different family units

> The advantages and disadvantages of belonging to a family

> Family jokes, anecdotes, memories

> Family festivals and celebrations

> Families in books

Share your ideas with other groups, taking note especially of the variety of ways of looking at 'The Family'.

You may wish to pursue some of your ideas through talk, reading, writing and drama.

On the Edge, Gillian Cross

We have chosen to focus on a thrilling new novel, full of drama and suspense in which at least **four** different viewpoints of the family are explored. The following extract introduces Jinny's family. (N.B. The 'Joe' mentioned is Jinny's father who is in his workshop during this time; 'Oz' is Jinny's eight-year-old brother.)

87

When she pushed open the kitchen door, all her questions and protests vanished immediately, swallowed up by chaos. Her mother was sitting at the big, scrubbed, wooden table with a mountain of runner beans in front of her, slicing desperately. And on either side of her was a furious, shouting child.

Oz was tugging at her right arm, putting her in severe danger of cutting herself. 'Mum, I'm *hollow*! I'll never live to be nine if you don't *feed* me! I've got this great pit inside me that's churning and rumbling and –'

On the other side, Louise, the baby, was lying on the floor in a basket, bellowing her head off. As Jinny stepped into the room, Bella put her knife down and yelled.

'*Will* you both stop it, you little monsters! You're driving me off my head!'

At the sound of her voice, Louise screamed even louder, turning purple in the face, and Bella whirled round. Making one of her huge, untidy gestures, she scooped the baby up and hugged her. 'There now! Did your rotten mother bawl at you? You're not a monster at all, are you? You're a dear, lovely little pig-baby.' She rubbed her nose against Louise's cheek. 'And you're starving to death. I'm a horrid, unnatural mother, aren't I? Yes? Yes!'

'*Yes!*' howled Oz.

Jinny stood still taking in the scene, deciding what she should do. Then she stepped forward.

'Honestly, Mum, she'll never shut up unless you feed her. You might as well give in now.'

'But the *beans!*' Bella ran her free hand through her thick, curly hair. 'The beans, the beans, the wretched *beans!* I've got to get this lot done today. There'll be more tomorrow and more the day after that. And if I don't get them done we'll all die of hunger in the winter.'

She pulled a face and let her head lurch dramatically sideways. Oz screeched and tugged at her hair.

'*I* won't starve to death in the winter. I'll have been dead for *months* by then!'

'Waa-aah!' screamed Louise.

Jinny took over. She knew that Bella was really enjoying herself, but the noise was unbearable.

'Look, you feed Louise. I'll give Oz a butty and then *I'll* do the beans.'

CHARACTERS IN FICTION: *On the Edge*, Gillian Cross

'Bless you, you're a dear little freckly angel!' Bella unbuttoned her blouse. 'Bread's in the crock and there's a bit of cheese in the larder.'

Jinny cut a huge doorstep of the heavy wholemeal bread, smeared it with butter and slammed a lump of crumbly cheese on top. Plugging Oz's mouth with that, she sat down at the table and picked up the knife, beginning to slice the first bean into neat slivers.

'Peace, perfect peace.' Bella smiled sentimentally and ran a finger over Louise's downy head. 'You're a great rescuer, Jin.'

'Have to be, don't I?' Jinny grinned rudely. 'It's a wonder we ever eat at all. This is such a madhouse.'

'Jolly, though.' Bella picked up a raw bean and began to chew it. 'Just think. If we'd stayed in London, we'd be a boring, ordinary family. Probably be driving off with a caravan for our boring holidays in the country. Pretending we knew how people in the country live. At least this is *real*.'

'So that's what real life is like,' Jinny said. 'No money and a mountain of runner beans. I always wondered.'

'Coo, you're ratty.' Bella smiled her big, sleepy smile. 'Been quarrelling with someone? Keith?'

'Not really,' said Jinny. Then she remembered something. 'Mum –'

'Mmm?'

'Who's Harriet Shakespeare?'

Bella munched at her bean. 'What on earth d'you want to know *that* for?'

'Oh nothing. It's just that – someone – laughed at me because I'd not heard of her.'

'Aha! I knew something had bitten you. Well, she's nothing exciting. A tele-lady. Sort of journalist, I suppose. I think she specializes in snooping round peculiar political groups. Finding out scare stories. Just the sort of person Joe can't stand.' She took another enormous bite of her bean. 'How did she come up?'

'Her son,' Jinny said. 'He's being held hostage in London. It was on the radio while I was in the Post Office.'

'*Don't* tell me!' Bella gave a wicked chuckle. 'Mrs Hollins grinned all over her face and said, "There's a terrible thing!" Aren't I right?'

Shifting viewpoints

But it is terrible, thought Jinny. *For the boy*. Then she remembered something, and she smiled after all. 'You're not quite right. It was worse than that. She said, "Think if it had been our Rachel!"'

'Oh!' said Bella longingly. '*Oh!* If *only*.' Her eyes met Jinny's and she gave such a loud shriek of laughter that the baby jerked an arm and knocked a landslide of beans on to the floor.

Talking

- Does this family remind you of any family you have met, heard of or read about?
- From this extract, what conclusions do you come to about the kind of family this is?
- What might be the advantages and disadvantages of being a teenager in this family?
- Discuss Bella's attitudes towards her own and other people's families in this extract.

Reading aloud

Working in small groups, pick out the dialogue in this extract and practise reading it aloud to bring out the humour in the situation and the attitudes of the three speakers – the baby just howls!

Remember that for reading aloud to be effective you have to be willing to take on the *viewpoint* of the character who is speaking, regardless of whether you are male or female.

The next extract introduces Keith Hollins' family. We have already picked up some clues about Mrs Hollins and her daughter, Rachel, from Bella and Jinny's conversation. What we, as readers, have to bear in mind is that this is *their* view of them, and that view is bound to be influenced by what *they* regard as an ideal family.

11.00 a.m.

Jinny was still running when she reached the edge of the village. She had to make herself stop so that she had a chance to get her breath back. It would be asking for trouble to arrive panting and upset if Rachel happened to be about.

But as she came up to the Post Office, she could see that it was all right. Rachel was busy. She was sitting on her wall again, but so were David and Harry Tansley and Andrew Walsh. All vying with each other to make clever comments and impress her. Rachel was being sweet and feminine, smiling at all of them and laughing at one joke in five. She barely looked as Jinny scuttled past towards the back door.

There was not even any need to knock. As she reached it, Mr Hollins came out, putting on his helmet. He gave her a strange glance, but he did not comment. Just pushed the door wider.

'Go on in, lass. Keith's in the lounge. *If* you can see him under all his muddle. See if you can get him to tidy up a bit before his Mam – *you* know.'

Jinny nodded. 'Yes. Thanks.' Her voice sounded squeaky and odd to her, but Mr Hollins did not seem to notice. He walked away and she made for the lounge door.

'*Keith!*'

He was sitting at the table with a huge heap of newspapers in front of him and more on the floor. Jinny was so relieved to see his heavy, solemn face that she launched herself forward.

'I've got to tell you, only it's so difficult to explain when I – oh Keith, it was *awful!*'

Once she started speaking, she began to cry, and her nose and her eyes streamed as her voice babbled on and on.

'– he was horrible and really I'd not done a thing to set him off, but he made me feel–'

Keith was not in the least put out. He coped with her, just as he had been coping ever since he was ten and she was a scared five year old, being bullied by the other children at school because of her southern accent. He stood up and let her crash against him, putting an arm round her while she wailed into the front of his jumper.

When he had given her a couple of minutes to get over the worst of it, he said, 'Tea.'

'Oh, you're right, and I'm sorry to come yelling in here, but it's shock I'm sure and –'

'Of course it's shock,' Keith said calmly. 'The whole side of your face is a right mess. What have you been up to?'

Jinny lifted a hand and touched her cheek. It was sore in some places and numb in others and her fingers came away with blood on them. 'I fell. Down the slope in Back Clough Dale. And then a man came and he said – he said –'

Keith pushed her down into a chair. 'It's soft to try and talk before you're over the shock. Here, drink this and wait till you're calmed down.'

He thrust his own mug of tea into her hand. Jinny pulled a face at the sweetness, but after a sip or two she felt less shaky. She reached out to put the mug down, but there was no space. The open newspapers covered every inch of the table. Automatically, she started to push them into a pile.

'You are a *slob*, Keith. You know your Mam'll go mad if she sees this lot. How anyone can be as clever as you and not *learn* –'

'Glad you're better.' Keith grinned at her and pulled away a copy of the *Sun*. 'Now let my work alone and tell us what's up.'

'It's –' Jinny felt her throat begin to tighten as she thought about what had happened. All at once, she was not so sure that she did want to talk about it. It would sound so thin. She turned back to the papers. 'Work? How's reading the papers *work?*'

'Tell you after.' Firmly, Keith took her hands away from *The Times* and the *Daily Express* and the *Guardian*. 'When you've pulled your head out of the sand. What is it, now? Tell Uncle Keith. Cow got foot and mouth? Handsome stranger passed by and broken your heart?'

Jinny smiled.

'Aha! It *is* the handsome stranger!'

''Course it's not. Why not listen if you're that keen to hear?'

Keith looked exaggeratedly solemn. 'My ears are flapping.' Putting his hands up on either side of his head, he waggled them.

'No, *really* listen.' Jinny twisted her hands together in her lap and stared down at them, working out where to start. Setting everything in order in her head. She began with hearing the people arrive at the cottage in the middle of the night. But she left out her reason for being out so

CHARACTERS IN FICTION: *On the Edge*, Gillian Cross

late. It was not fair to tell Keith things like that, not with his father being a policeman. He noticed the gap, of course, and she saw him blink, but he did not say anything.

'Then yesterday morning I met the woman. In the shop. She –' Jinny hesitated. But there was no point in trying to explain what the Hare-woman was like. Better to stick to facts. 'She told two lies. Said that her son had a noisy fall when they came. Noisy enough to waken the village. And that they went straight to bed after. But it wasn't like that. None of it.'

*

As she let herself out, she heard Mrs Hollins come through from the shop and she suddenly remembered that she had not made Keith tidy up. Now it was too late to do anything, and the explosion was audible all through the house.

'Keith Hollins! You're like a baby, scattering papers everywhere. And it's no good trying to call it work. Reading newspapers is never work. Get them picked up at once!'

Keith mumbled something apologetic and Jinny squirmed. She knew just how he would be looking. Stupid and shambling and guilty.

'And when you've done that,' Mrs Hollins shouted, 'you can just take yourself upstairs and make your bed again. Call that *made*? A six-year-old could do better. I've taken all the covers off and put them on the floor.'

For a moment, Jinny was tempted to go back and help Keith. He was so *soft*. He never stood up to his mother. It was nothing to her that he was clever and kind and gentle. All she could see was his untidiness. And because that was what she saw, it was what he saw himself. It wasn't *fair*.

But then she remembered that she was annoyed with him herself, because he had made nothing out of her mystery and her worries. So she closed the door and went back to her own house. And the beans.

Improvisation Improvise a scene in which all the members of the Hollins' family are present, e.g. at a family meal.

Use all the information provided in *any* of the extracts to help you to create convincing roles.

93

Think about Mr Hollins' work as a policeman and Mrs Hollins being in charge of the Post Office when you are developing the conversation, which could include comments about people in the community.

At some point in the improvisation, Keith introduces the subject of the 'Message' from the Free People (see the extract on p. 99) which he has cut out of the newspaper.

If you decide to share your group's work with the rest of the class, you will need to think carefully about the *shape* of your scene.

Note down a few key phrases which will help you to sustain your roles and introduce new topics of conversation.

Decide *when* and *how* to end the scene. One interesting possibility might be the arrival of another person in the story.

Our third extract introduces Tug's 'family'.

Day Three – Tuesday 9th August

8.00 a.m.

Tug crouched on his bed, watching the door. Waiting. He had not slept since the Man and the Woman walked out, after that first visit, hours ago. The noise and the fear, jangling together in his head, made it impossible to relax and he had no idea what time it was. He knew there had been a night, because all through it he had watched the dark skylight, spattered with stars, but his watch said eleven o'clock on the fourth of March and he was certain it was wrong. Or almost certain.

He was very hungry and thirsty, but he had not even touched the water in the plastic jug. He had just stayed on his bed, alert and tense, waiting for Them to come back. Fighting his headache and the monotonous, obsessive beat of the band while he tried to *think*. Now all his questions were ready and his eyes were fixed on the latch.

When it finally moved, it was almost an anti-climax. The Man let himself in, with a louder burst of sound as the door opened.

... the KEEL row ....

Walking over to the bed, he looked Tug up and down, taking his time. Somehow it was impossible to speak first.

'Sleep well?' he said at last.

'No.' Tug's voice came out as a croak from a dry, sore throat.

'Have some water.' The Man nodded at the jug. Seeing Tug's hesitation, he grinned slowly. 'It won't poison you.' He crossed to the chest of drawers, picked up the jug and drank from it. Then he held it out.

I'm not taking anything from you, Tug wanted to say. *Not until you tell me what's going on.* Only – the dryness in his throat was almost unbearable and he did not see how there *could* be anything wrong with the water.

The Man shrugged.

Sliding off the bed, Tug padded across the floor and took the jug. He did not put it down until it was almost empty. Then he said, 'Don't you think it's time you –'

'Sit down on the bed,' said the Man.

'But I don't want –' began Tug.

Then he saw, from the Man's faint frown, that he was being unwise. He went over to the bed and sat on it. When he was safely there, the Man opened the door, stepped through it and bent down, still watching Tug over his shoulder. It was impossible to see what he was doing, but his hand reached out along the floor outside.

And suddenly the music stopped.

The relief was so enormous that Tug's ears tingled with it and he flopped back against the wall as though his muscles had been disconnected. Beautiful, magic silence. It was not spoilt, even by the smile on the Man's face which showed that he perfectly understood the lightness, the freedom from struggling against the noise.

Then, in the quiet, another pair of feet began to climb the stairs. Slowly and carefully, each clack of a heel sounding extraordinarily loud. Tug leaned forward as the door opened wider and the Woman walked in with a tray. She stood for a moment, letting him see what was on it.

'Breakfast,' she said.

It was a dream breakfast. Bacon and egg and sausage and beans and tomatoes. All steaming hot. A rack of toast with marmalade and butter in dishes. And a big mug of tea. Tug had never realized before that people's mouths really watered. Now it was all he could do not to dribble. He stared at the tray, and the Woman went on standing by the door holding it.

'Well?' he said at last. 'Isn't it for me?'

She nodded. 'Oh yes, it's for you all right.'

'Do you want me to come and fetch it?'

'No. I'll give it to you. But what do you say, first?'

As if I was a snotty little kid, thought Tug in disgust. It seemed ridiculous. But – what did it matter?

'Thank you,' he said.

'Thank you –' she left the words hanging and raised her eyebrows.

Guessing games? When he was starving? Perhaps it was a sort of torture. Bewildered, Tug looked from one to the other. 'I don't get it. Thank you – what?'

'You usually call her something,' said the Man. Softly and dangerously.

An idea of what they wanted began to seep into Tug's head. And yet – were they *serious*? In spite of the colour of his hair, in spite of the madness of everything, he had not quite been able to believe it. And even now he played ignorant.

'I don't know what you're talking about. *What* do I usually call her?'

It was the Woman who answered. 'Ma,' she said. 'You call me Ma.'

It caught him off balance. He had been bracing himself for her to say 'Mum', ready to mock at it in his head because she didn't look like anyone's Mum. But – Ma? He looked at her as she stood there, alert and threatening, poised on the balls of her feet. Ma? Perhaps.

'Your breakfast's getting cold,' she said, watching him. But he was not ready to give in yet. He turned to stare at the Man.

'And I suppose I call you Pa,' he muttered. Rudely. Disbelievingly.

The Man smiled calmly, as though he had been waiting for just that question. 'No. You could, but you don't. You call me Doyle.'

Doyle ... Ma ... Tug's eyes flickered from one to the

other. It was complicated. It almost had the gritty feel of truth. Suddenly he bunched his fists and screwed his eyes up. 'You're both *mad*!' he shouted. 'You're mad, you're mad! You can't really expect me to believe this rubbish! Why don't you tell me what's going on and –'

The door crashed shut. He opened his eyes again and saw that the Woman had walked out, taking his breakfast with her.

'Stupid,' said Doyle softly. 'You've upset her.'

'But –' Tug stammered, and then stopped. They couldn't be going to starve him to death. Not just for that. Could they?

'Funny how strange mothers are.' Doyle's voice was as light as a thought. He tilted his head towards the door and Tug heard the sound of footsteps coming up the stairs again. 'I shouldn't risk another upset,' Doyle murmured.

Tug heard the Woman climbing, slowly and carefully. Carrying a tray. Eerily, as though he were watching a replay of his life, he saw the door open. She stepped inside and stood still.

The food looked just as hot and delicious as it had before. Tug could smell it from where he was sitting.

'Breakfast,' said the Woman.

Tug looked sideways at Doyle, but Doyle did not speak. Then he looked towards the food on the tray and thought. He did not understand why they were playing this charade, but playing charades would not kill him. Not like starvation. And what did a word matter? He did not even use that word for his mother.

He took a deep breath.

'Thank you – Ma.'

The Woman did not smile or look triumphant. She simply stepped across the room, laid the tray on his lap and walked back to the door. And Tug felt as though something had drained out of him, leaving him small and empty.

Doyle stepped after her on to the landing, but when he was outside, he turned and smiled slowly, looking straight into Tug's eyes.

'Have a good breakfast – Philip.'

'I'm *not* Philip,' Tug yelled. 'And you're *not* my parents!'

But the door had already closed. Feeling sick, Tug pushed the tray off his lap and walked over to the

Shifting viewpoints

wardrobe. Opening it, he stared into the mirror and the hateful, strange face with the black hair stared back at him. But it was not as strange as it had been the first time he saw it. Somehow, in the time in between, his brain had adjusted and now when he looked at it he saw his own face at once.

His first, angry urge was to smash the glass. To beat at it with his fist until the face was smashed into thousands of pieces. But the first thump had no effect at all and, losing heart, he changed his mind. He leaned forward and began to breathe on the glass. The face disappeared in a misty blur and Tug wrote across it, scrawling the capitals with his forefinger.

I'M NOT PHILIP
I'M TUG

But even before he had finished, the mist evaporated and the letters vanished, leaving the black-haired face staring angrily back at him.

And then the music started again. It was a double torture, taking his mind off guard and shattering the precious silence.

As readers of this extract you are expected to share Tug's uncertainty about what is going on. It is what the writer intends you to feel at this point in the story. At the same time it is essential that you make guesses about the strange behaviour of the Man and the Woman and the reasons for it.

Talking

- Share any ideas you have about the situation described in this extract, the characters involved and their behaviour.
- Can you make any links between this and the other extracts?

One way of becoming a more confident *reader* is to work with the material as a *writer*. You should find that creating your own play script for radio will help you to appreciate the power and the drama in this part of the story.

CHARACTERS IN FICTION: *On the Edge*, Gillian Cross

Talking and reading aloud

Discuss how you might adapt this scene for radio. You will need to think about and make detailed notes on:
- setting the scene and creating the sinister atmosphere;
- how to present Tug's thoughts and feelings before the dialogue begins – you could use a narrator, but do consider other possibilities;
- where to add more dialogue, e.g. to let your listeners know that it is 'a dream breakfast' to Tug who is extremely hungry;
- the use of sound effects and the order in which they are to be recorded;
- the use of *silence* in both building up and breaking tension in this scene.

Writing and reading aloud

Write your first draft.

Try out your play script; be prepared to redraft those parts which are not convincing. If you decide to go on working towards a 'polished' presentation, you may need expert help with making a master tape of sound effects.

Now read our fourth extract from *On the Edge*.

A Message from the Free People to their Comrades Still in Prison

Comrades, it is time to wake and see your chains!

WOMEN open your eyes and see how you are chained to husbands and children. All the equal opportunities in the world cannot save you from the demands of your families.
THERE MUST BE A DIFFERENT PATTERN.

MEN open your eyes and see how you are chained to the capitalist system by the needs of your wives and children. As long as men have families, capitalists will be able to exploit them.
THERE MUST BE A DIFFERENT PATTERN.
CHILDREN open your eyes and see how you are chained to the needs and desires of your parents. And while they force you to be what you do not want to be, they are also teaching you how to be parents. Shudder when you understand that you, in your turn, will humiliate your aged parents and bully and deform your children.
THERE MUST BE A DIFFERENT PATTERN.

Shifting viewpoints

Talking and writing

Work in pairs. You are members of the Free People group and you are speaking at a public meeting. Prepare your speech making use of the 'Message' published by the Free People. You should develop the argument by giving examples to support the points you make. You should suggest, as Free People, what 'different pattern' you have in mind.

Now you are members of a 'Save the Family' group. Use the 'Message' from the Free People as your model. Write your own 'Message' in the form of a pamphlet to be handed out at a public meeting.

The following poster, designed by an artist called Aneurin Edwards, is based on the 'Message' from 'Free People'.

Drawing

Design and draw your own poster as part of a publicity campaign being organised by one of the groups.

100

Work sharing Prepare the classroom for a public meeting at which the topic for discussion is 'The Role of the Family in Modern Society'.

Choose two people to present the views of the 'Free People' and two to present those of the 'Save the Family' group.

Appoint a neutral chairperson who will introduce each speaker in turn and conduct the discussion afterwards.

Any publicity in the form of pamphlets and posters could be displayed or distributed at the meeting.

Remember that, as members of the general public, you must give all the speakers a chance to present their points of view. Any questions you wish to ask or statements you wish to make should be addressed to the chairperson at the end of the formal part of the meeting.

DRAMA

A Game of Soldiers, Jan Needle

Jan Needle wrote a three-part play for Thames Television's programme 'Middle English', in which he is very much concerned with the shifting viewpoints of his young characters.

A Game Of Soldiers is set against the background of the Falklands war of 1982. All the action takes place on the island at a time when the Argentinian troops are retreating.

The characters are:

Michael: He is twelve or thirteen, wearing jeans, rubber boots, camouflage jacket and a bush hat. He has a small clasp knife that he plays with a lot.

Sarah: She is slightly older than Michael and wears an ordinary anorak, jeans, rubber boots and a scarf.

Thomas: About eight, dressed in boots, jeans, anorak and woolly hat. Frequently the butt of Michael's sarcasm because he is so young. Sarah tries to protect him for the same reason.

The soldier: Aged sixteen to seventeen, injured and dirty. He is dressed in shabby military gear and carries a self-loading rifle.

We take up their story immediately after the children have found an injured Argentinian deserter who has taken refuge in a sheep hut. They go to their den to decide what to do.

Scene 6

The sea den with the old radio telephone set. The children are having a serious discussion.

THOMAS   But **why** aren't we going to tell anyone? We've got to. When my Dad finds out he'll **murder** me.

SARAH   He won't find out, though, will he? Unless you tell him, Big Mouth. And even you wouldn't be that stupid, would you?

MICHAEL   I wouldn't be so sure of that. But I tell you this, Thomas. If your Dad does find out, we'll know who told him. And then **we'll** murder you!

THOMAS   But why can't we tell the grown-ups? What are **we** going to do with him in any case?

SARAH   Because he said so, didn't he? You heard him, didn't you? He said we weren't to tell the soldiers. You heard him.

MICHAEL   He was too busy pooing himself with fright!

SARAH   Don't be filthy, Michael. Listen Thomas, it's a **secret**. It's got to be, that's all. If the soldiers found him, I don't know what would happen. Or some of them hotheads, like Mr Gregory, say.

THOMAS   They'd put him down like a sick sheep. My Dad said so. The farmers ganged together at Foster's Landing when they found them others. Execution squad. It's dangerous, though. In case they win the war.

MICHAEL   Who? The enemy? Don't be ruddy daft, of course they won't! Against the British! You unpatriotic little swine!

DRAMA: *A Game of Soldiers*, Jan Needle

SARAH   Anyway, whatever **really** happened at Foster's Landing, it's not the point. Whoever found him, it wouldn't turn out good. He might get treated. . . . Well, he said we weren't to tell.

MICHAEL [*slyly, after a pause*]   We didn't say we wouldn't though, did we Sarah? We don't **owe** him anything, do we?

THOMAS   Owe him anything! He'd kill us if he got the chance! He's the enemy.

MICHAEL   Exactly. We don't owe him a thing. Right, Sarah?

SARAH   Well we do owe him something, surely? I mean, he **didn't** shoot us, did he? And he could have done, couldn't he? If he'd wanted to?

THOMAS   You're stupid you are, Sarah. Of course he'd kill us. It's his job.

MICHAEL   What do you mean, anyway? We owe him 'something'? What could we possibly owe him?

SARAH [*confused*]   Well. You know. I mean, he **is** a human being. We ought at least to get him food and water. I think he's injured. He looked terrible. I think he must have been shot or something. You know.

THOMAS   If he was shot, it was our side that did it, wasn't it? If he was shot it was because he was shooting our lot. He's a murderer, stands to reason. He's the enemy.

MICHAEL   Exactly. He's the enemy. He's a prisoner of war. Don't you get it yet? Sarah? Don't you get it yet why he's got to be our secret?

SARAH   No. I don't know what you're talking about. He's a human being, that's all, and he's injured. We've got to bring him food. What are **you** on about?

Pause.

MICHAEL   Look Sarah. Look at it this way. He's the enemy, right? Which **means** if you think about it, he's out to kill the lot of us in the end. He's here to ruinate, destroy.

THOMAS   He's a rapist and despoiler.

MICHAEL   Shut up Thomas, yeah. He's a ruinator, fair enough. Look Sarah, we didn't ask them in, they just arrived and mucked the whole place up. They've smashed the radios, and the phones, and they've killed sheep and messed up lots of houses. They've put down mines an'all. On the fields. And on the beaches. They've wrecked the place.

THOMAS My Dad says it's wrecked for good. Even when the Brits have seen them off. Even when the Gurkhas have slit their throats and chucked them in the sea. It'll be years before it's safe again. The mines are everywhere. They've ruinated everything. It'll be years.

MICHAEL He's right see, Sarah? There's no denying it. Your little 'human being' up there in the hut – he's just a bloody murderer. It serves him right if he's been hit. It serves him right to suffer. He's a prisoner of war. Ours. **Our** prisoner of war. D'you see it now?

SARAH So what are you suggesting, Michael? What d'you say we should do? Have you got a plan?

Quite a pause.

MICHAEL We've got to kill him, Sarah. We've got to do our bit. We've got to show the grown-ups that we care. It's got to be a proper execution.

SARAH *stands up. Her mouth drops open.*

THOMAS Hey! Hey Michael, that's a good idea. Then my Dad can't tell me off, can he? Hey, that's a good idea.

SARAH [*quietly*] You're joking, aren't you Michael? You're trying to pull my leg.

MICHAEL [*staring at her face*] No Sarah. I'm serious. Look, either way he dies. If we leave him, he dies of cold and starves. If we tell on him, he dies, the hotheads get him – Tom's Dad and Mr Gregory. My way, we do our bit. We do our bit towards the war, we help. It's our duty, Sarah. It's our duty to the war.

SARAH *moves to leave.*

SARAH Sometimes I wonder about you, Michael. You're insane.

MICHAEL He's going to die anyway, Sarah. You know he is. And if you don't agree it's our duty, you're not a patriot. [SARAH *leaves*] You're a traitor!

DRAMA: *A Game of Soldiers*, Jan Needle

THOMAS   Sarah! Come back!

MICHAEL   Leave her be, Tom, leave her be. She'll do it in the end. Just let her stew a bit.

THOMAS, *torn, moves slowly away.*

THOMAS   I'm going after her. I won't be long.

MICHAEL   [*as* THOMAS *leaves*]   She'll do it in the end. Just let her stew.

He moves to radio telephone and winds the handle.

MICHAEL   Patrol to base. Patrol to base. I read you loud and clear. Destroy the enemy. Destroy. I read you loud and clear. Roger and out.

Scene 7

Another part of the moor. The children have been arguing. SARAH, *very cool, is sitting.* MICHAEL, *frustrated, has clearly been haranguing her.*

SARAH   [*quietly*]   You can stand there ranting until you're blue in the face, Michael. But it won't make any difference. Unless you agree, I'm not swearing. And that's flat.

MICHAEL   But it's stupid, that's all. If we're going to kill him, why bother? Food and blankets and a fire! It's ridiculous.

SARAH   And so are you, Michael. Apart from anything else it might even make it easier, mightn't it? Apart from anything else it might make him easier to approach. He **has** got a rifle, you know.

THOMAS   Yeah. She might have a point Michael. He might think we want to be his friends.

MICHAEL   Oh shut up, you little weed. You just keep out of this.

SARAH   [*to Thomas, sarcastically*]   You can tell he sees it's sense, Tommy. He's shouting at you!

MICHAEL *makes a threatening gesture at her and she gives him a look: Oh grow up.*

MICHAEL   Anyway, how do I know you'll keep your promise? If you go back to your house for blankets and stuff, how do I know you won't tell?

SARAH   Because I'll have **sworn**, you ratbag! God you're brainless, you are.

THOMAS   I won't tell neither, Michael. I can get the matches easy. I've got them hidden in my drawer. My Dad'd kill me if he knew.

MICHAEL   I don't blame him, you're so thick. It's a wonder you haven't burnt the house down ages ago.

SARAH   Just a little fire, warm him up. A blanket for his legs, maybe a cup of tea and a sandwich.

MICHAEL   And then we kill him?

SARAH *looks shifty.*

MICHAEL [*insistent*]   And then we kill him? Right? You'll swear?

SARAH [*brazen*]   Yeah. If it comes to. . . .

MICHAEL   That's it, see! You're trying to slide out!

SARAH [*shouts*]   I am not. I'll swear. And if it comes to it. All right.

MICHAEL   It will, Sarah, it bloody will. And you'll have **sworn**. Got it? You'll have bloody **sworn**.

SARAH *looks up at him with contempt on her face.*

SARAH   Yes, Michael. I understand. I'll have sworn. Now dry up about it, eh?

THOMAS [*to himself, preoccupied. He's a little worried*]   She'll never catch me if I'm quiet. They're in the second drawer. She'll never catch me.

MICHAEL *is gazing at* SARAH, *who is still sitting, picking at a thread. He is forced to make his decision.*

MICHAEL   Right. We swear. Come on. Everyone make a ring. Come **on**, Sarah.

SARAH *stands, and they form a star, with one hand touching in the centre. They walk one circuit in one direction, then reverse, change hands, and walk one circuit in the other direction. Then they hold hands, facing each other in a ring.*

CHANT   One, two, three – SWEAR.

DRAMA: *A Game of Soldiers*, Jan Needle

MICHAEL   My name is Michael. I swear.

Abruptly they do the star ritual once more, then form the ring.

CHANT   One, two, three – SWEAR.

THOMAS   My name is Thomas. I swear.

Repeat star and ring.

CHANT   One, two, three – SWEAR.

SARAH   My name is Sarah. I swear.

She immediately breaks the circle and starts to walk off.

MICHAEL [*following*]   Sarah! Where are you going?

SARAH   Where do you think, stupid? To be sick? I'm going to make some sandwiches.

She has gone. MICHAEL, *almost off, shouts after her.*

MICHAEL   Well don't forget, Sarah. You can't go back on a swear. And that's flat.

He leaves, followed by THOMAS.

Talking and reading aloud

- As you read through the two scenes notice:
  - the way in which each character expresses a point of view and develops it;
  - any apparent changes in attitude in any of the characters;
  - the playwright's use of *pause* and change of *pace* from the quick argumentative exchanges at the beginning of scene six to the 'ritual oath swearing' at the end of scene seven.
- Talk about the differences in attitude between Michael and Sarah. Do you think any of them can be explained by the fact that Sarah is a girl and slightly older than Michael?
- Choose two statements made by each character which sums up her/his present attitude towards the war and the soldier.
- What experiences might cause a change in their attitudes?
- Why do you think Sarah agreed to 'swear' to the killing?
- Look at the part played by Thomas in these two scenes. How does he add to the conflict in the situation?
- At this point in the play what are the options open to the children?

Improvise   Improvise one short scene in which you take up one of the options. You could introduce other characters if you wish.

In Jan Needle's play script, whilst Sarah and Thomas are fetching supplies, Michael offers to stand guard over the soldier.

At one dramatic moment he has the opportunity to shoot the unconscious soldier but is unable to do so. Shortly afterwards, Sarah and Thomas return to find Michael listening to a cassette tape belonging to the young Argentinian.

Scene 12

The sheep hut. MICHAEL *is crouched beside the* SOLDIER, *who is sitting with his back to the wall.* MICHAEL *has the cassette headphones on, listening hard. The* SOLDIER *is watching him almost anxiously.* MICHAEL *wants to please, wants to show friendship, but is puzzled. He takes off the headphones and smiles helplessly.*

SOLDIER   Madre . . . . Is . . . mother . . . . She says . . . when come home . . . .

MICHAEL *solemnly hands back the headset. He jumps when he hears the others.*

SARAH [*outside the shelter*]   Michael? Quick. We've got some food. [*They come in*] You've got a fire going!

MICHAEL [*shamefaced*]   Yeah. He had some matches in a tin.

SARAH [*briskly*]   Good. Quick, get this round his legs.

MICHAEL   It's a message from his mum . . . she wants him to come home. Look Sarah . . . we can't . . . I mean. I tried to shoo . . . I got the rifle but. . . .

SARAH [*half laughs*]   You daft devil, of course you couldn't. Look, shift! I've got some sandwiches and a kettle full of water. No milk though. Thomas spilled it all.

MICHAEL   You're not furious? The oath and that? I thought. . . .

SARAH   Oh do stop wittering. Just get that blanket down. We understand completely. [*Sarcastic*] **Don't** we, Thomas?

DRAMA: *A Game of Soldiers*, Jan Needle

THOMAS *flounces into a corner.* SARAH *undoes the sandwiches.*
MICHAEL *lays the blanket over the* SOLDIER'S *legs*

MICHAEL   What's up with **him**?

SARAH [*putting kettle on fire*]   That's the bad news. He's told, that's what. He's told his rotten mother. I nearly killed him.

MICHAEL   He's **told**! What does that . . . ? I mean. . . . Oh glory, Sarah! What are we going to do?

SARAH [*giving sandwiches to* SOLDIER]   Here, Mister. Eat some food. It's corned beef. You'll like that, won't you?

SOLDIER *tries to smile. He raises sandwich slowly to his mouth. He looks sick.*

SOLDIER   Thank you. Good children. Your friend . . . good boy.

He bites slowly, carefully, But SARAH *has turned back to* MICHAEL.

SARAH   He says his mother doesn't believe him but it's not the point. He says he ran away, she sent him to his room. But they'll be looking soon, they're bound to be. [*Nodding at the* SOLDIER] We've got to save him, Michael.

MICHAEL   Who'll be looking? Mr Wyatt and his friends? Or the army?

SARAH   The army'd be all right. They've got rules. They'd make him into a prisoner. But if Thomas's Dad. . . . If some of the hotheads. . . . You know. Like at Foster's Landing.

MICHAEL   You don't think they'd actually. . . . You don't believe they really . . . when they found those others? Killed . . . ?

SARAH   Ssh! Look, Michael, no. People don't really . . . it's just a crazy. . . . But they'd . . . they might be angry. Cruel. He's just a boy on his own. We've got to get him somewhere safe. We've got to.

SOLDIER [*he has been listening. He has only taken a few bites. He is holding his neck*]   Army? You talk the army? Not tell soldiers, no? Please. Not tell soldiers.

He is distressed.

MICHAEL   All right, Maria. You'll be all right. Don't you worry, eat your sandwiches.

The SOLDIER *does not eat. He stares at them. He swallows painfully.*

SARAH   Maria?

MICHAEL   That's his name. I think.

THOMAS   But that's a girl's name.

MICHAEL   Oh shut up. Look. Come outside. Everybody.

They move away from the SOLDIER *and look down the moor. He is straining to overhear. They do not want to distress him.*

MICHAEL   Thomas, you've got one more chance. Go down to the bottom of the moor to watch. If you see anyone moving, **anyone**, get back here. **Anyone**. [THOMAS *makes as if to move.* MICHAEL *grabs his arm.*] And Tom. Don't let them see which way you go. Under **any** circumstances. If you let us down once more, you're for it. Understand?

THOMAS *looks at his face and flinches. He nods.* MICHAEL *shoves him and he runs. They watch him go careering down the hill.*

The SOLDIER *has tried to get closer. He is on his knees.* SARAH *hurries to him.* MICHAEL *remains outside.*

SARAH [*supporting him, trying to get him to move*]   Can you move? Can you move at all? You've got to move, you've got to. We've got to hide you from the men.

MICHAEL [*joins her*]   We've got to hide him from bloody Thomas. **Move**, Maria, move.

SOLDIER   Soldiers come? Not tell soldiers.

SARAH   Not the soldiers, no. It's farmers. They're angry. They have guns. The soldiers are all right. We've got to hide you from the men.

SOLDIER [*makes a groaning, crying noise. Doubles over even further*]   No. Hurting. Ah. Hurting.

He sinks onto his haunches. They support him, distraught.

SARAH   Lie back. Lie back. Oh Michael, he's in agony.

MICHAEL [*gives up*]   Yeah. Come on. Come on, Maria. You lie back. You're not going anywhere. Lie back.

As he helps the SOLDIER *lie down once more and covers him,* SARAH *goes to the doorway. She stares across the moors.* MICHAEL *joins her.*

DRAMA: *A Game of Soldiers*, Jan Needle

SARAH   We should call the soldiers in ourselves. Quickly. It's the only hope. They'll give him drugs and stuff. He'll be a prisoner of war. They'll put him on a stretcher in a helicopter. It's the only hope.

MICHAEL   But he's terrified of them. It must be the enemy propaganda. He must believe that the British Army. . . . It's crazy, Sarah. We're scared of the farmers, and he's scared of the soldiers. And we'll **both** be wrong, it's stupid, stupid, stupid. It's only games, like thinking we could . . . you know. It's all crazy.

Talking and improvisation

- In pairs, talk about what might have happened between Michael and the soldier which has led to Michael's change in attitude towards him. How do you think they managed to communicate?
- Improvise your scene so that:
  – your 'audience' can believe in the change;
  – it provides a natural link between the 'swearing' and the beginning of scene twelve where 'Michael wants to show friendship'.
- Improvise a scene between Sarah and Thomas in which she discovers that he has 'told his rotten mother'. (You might find it embarrassing 'to act' as an eight year old, but remember that you are trying to show Thomas' *attitude*, his thoughts and feelings – you do not need to 'shrink' and put on a childish voice!)

Writing

- Complete this scene in order to provide an appropriate ending to the whole play.
- Imagine that you are either Michael or Sarah and that you have a penfriend in England. Write a letter describing some of the incidents that happened during the war and your thoughts and feelings about them.

VERSE

Thaw, Edward Thomas

In the play *A Game of Soldiers*, Jan Needle used three characters and many pages of dialogue to voice different and changing viewpoints towards the problem posed by the finding of the young, enemy soldier.

Edward Thomas, in his poem *Thaw*, shows a poet's skill in condensing meaning and three viewpoints into only four lines of verse:

Over the land freckled with snow half-thawed
The speculating rooks at their nests cawed
And saw from elm-tops, delicate as flower of grass,
What we below could not see, Winter pass.

Below is an artist's impression of two of the viewpoints expressed in the poem:

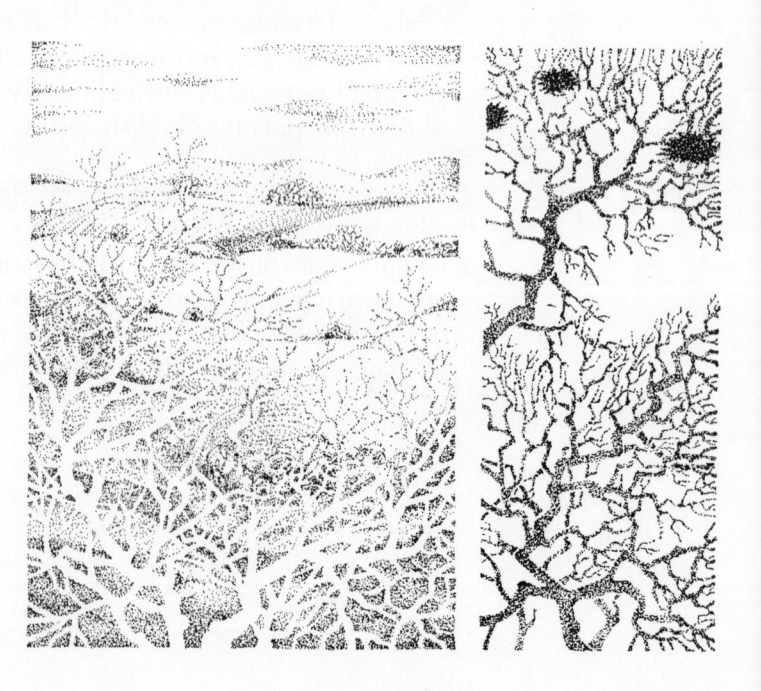

VERSE: *The Climb and the Dream*, Vernon Scannell

The third viewpoint, one that we often overlook when reading a poem, is that of the *poet*.

In this particular poem, as well as describing a landscape as the thaw begins, Thomas is suggesting that by using our imaginations we can 'see' things that we would not normally be able to see. He, the poet is able to 'become' the rooks in the elm-tops as well as the human being on the ground.

Reading and writing

- Read the poem aloud several times, enjoying particularly the sounds the words make.

Prepositions, such as 'over', 'under', 'inside', 'outside', 'above' and 'below', immediately suggest that there are different angles from which we can view the world in which we live. In his poem Thomas uses 'over' and 'below' to establish his viewpoints.

- Write a short poem beginning each verse with a different preposition.
- Using two contrasting prepositions, (e.g. 'inside', 'outside') write a four-line poem.

The Climb and the Dream, Vernon Scannell

The poet, like the storyteller, can choose to stand back and view events as if he were an observer, that is, writing in the third person. This is the viewpoint taken by Vernon Scannell in this poem.

The boy had never seen the tree before;
He thought it was a splendid one to climb,
The branches strong enough to take far more
Than his slight weight; and, while they did not rhyme
In perfect echoes of each other's shape,
They were arranged in useful patterns which
He found as thrilling as a fire-escape.
Now was his chance! He hopped across the ditch
And wriggled underneath the rusty wire,

Shifting viewpoints

And then he found himself confronted by
The lofty challenge, suddenly much higher
Now he was at its foot. He saw the sky
Through foliage and branches, broken like
A pale blue china plate. He leapt and clung
To the lowest branch and swung from left to right,
Then heaved himself astride the swaying rung.
With cautious hands and feet he made a start
From branch to branch; dust tickled in his throat.
He smelt the dark green scent of leaf and bark;
Malicious thorny fingers clutched his coat
And once clawed at his forehead, drawing blood.
Sweat drenched his aching body, blurred his eyes,
But he climbed up and up until he stood
Proud on the highest bough and, with surprise,
Looked down to see the shrunken fields and streams
As if his climb had re-created them;
And he was sure that, often, future dreams
Would bring this vision back to him. But then
A sudden darkening came upon the sky,
He felt the breeze grow burlier and chill,
Joy drained away. And then he realised why:
This was a tree he'd scaled, and not a hill –
The journey down would not be easier
But much more difficult than his ascent:
The foothold surfaces seemed greasier
And less accessible, and he had spent
Much of his strength, was very close to tears,
And sick with fear, yet knew he must go down.
The thing he dreamt about in after-years
Was not the moment when he wore the crown
Of gold achievement on the highest bough
Above the common world of strife and pain,
But the ordeal of dark descent, and how
He sobbed with joy to reach safe earth again.

Reading and talking

■ In pairs or small groups, read the poem aloud or quietly to yourselves. Remember that close attention to the title and the punctuation will help you to understand the poem.

VERSE: *The Climb and the Dream*, Vernon Scannell

- What do you find interesting about the 'shape' of the poem?
- Look at the poem closely. If the poet had written it in separate verses, where do you think he would have made the breaks? Why do you think he decided to write it in its present form?
- Imagine that this is one dramatic event in a film you are making. What instructions would you give to the camera crew and your boy actor in order to capture:
  – the setting;
  – the boy's movements before he gets to the tree and during the climb;
  – changes of mood and pace;
  – his 'dream'?
  We have included a production sheet (p. 116) to help you with some technical terms.
- At some time in the future, friends are swapping stories about their childhood. Each member of the group should choose one vivid memory to share; ask one person (girl or boy) to re-tell the story of *The Climb and the Dream*.

Writing

Take one of the childhood anecdotes that you have listened to in your group and re-tell it in the third person. Try to include any changes in mood, feelings and attitude as described by the person telling the story.

As the *writer* you might also wish to express a viewpoint by commenting on the behaviour of your main character.

Shifting viewpoints

Production Sheet

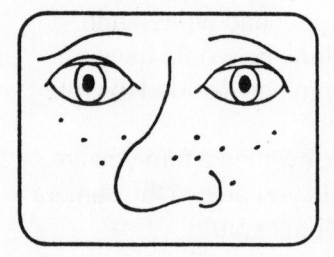

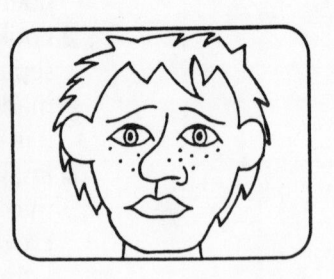

E.C.U. EXTREME CLOSE UP
FOR REVEALING DETAIL

V.C.U. VERY CLOSE UP
MID FOREHEAD TO ABOVE CHIN

B.C.U. BIG CLOSE UP
HEAD FILLS THE SCREEN

C.U. CLOSE UP
FROM SPACE ABOVE HEAD TO UPPER CHEST

X.L.S. OR W/S — EXTRA LONG SHOT OR WIDE SHOT
A DISTANT VIEWPOINT

M.C.U. MEDIUM CLOSE UP
CUTS BODY AT ARMPIT

M.S. MEDIUM SHOT
CUTS BODY JUST BELOW WAIST

M.L.S. MEDIUM LONG SHOT
ENTIRE BODY + AREA TOP & BOTTOM

L.S. LONG SHOT
BODY TAKES UP 3/4 TO 1/3 OF SCREEN HEIGHT

VERSE: *Take One Home for the Kiddies*, Philip Larkin

Take One Home for the Kiddies,
Philip Larkin

It is quite likely that one of your childhood memories centres around an animal. In the following short poem, Philip Larkin uses his own and another 'voice' to express a very strong point of view about keeping pets.

On shallow straw, in shadeless glass,
Huddled by empty bowls, they sleep;
No dark, no dam, no earth, no grass –
Mam, get us one of them to keep.

Living toys are something novel,
But it soon wears off somehow.
Fetch the shoe-box, fetch the shovel –
Mam, we're playing funerals now.

Reading and talking

- Practise reading the poem aloud emphasising the two 'voices'.
  Inverted commas have been omitted. Why do you think the poet decided not to put them in?
- What feelings does the poet hope to arouse in his reader? How far does the title, choice of words and introduction of another 'voice' help him to achieve this?

Drawing

- Think back to the picture book *Come Away From The Water, Shirley* at the beginning of this chapter. Here is a double-page opening. Draw pictures which illustrate the poet's words and point of view:

Mam, get us one of them to keep	Mam, we're playing funerals now

- Using the ideas from the poem, draw a poster as part of an R.S.P.C.A. publicity campaign.

4 Time passes

In this chapter we shall look at another dimension of your reading: how authors choose to indicate the passing of time.

Brainstorming In groups, do a brainstorming exercise on the word TIME.

For this activity you will need a large sheet of paper and a pencil. Appoint one person to listen to all the ideas and to jot them down.

After you have written down all the ideas share them with other groups.

Group all your suggestions into 'Time Boxes':

sayings, proverbs		historical time
	fantasy and dream time	
measuring time		time remembered
time future		games and rhymes

Add any further suggestions to these boxes and accept ideas for more headings if needed.

One heading which would cover all those already mentioned is the title we have given to this chapter. Even in the simplest picture book for very young children quite difficult concepts to do with time are introduced. It would be useful to borrow a collection of picture books from your library, if you do not have any in your own school, and to look closely at them for the way in which they help children's understanding of time.

We have chosen three children's picture books to illustrate some of the points.

PICTURE BOOKS
Clocks and More Clocks, Pat Hutchins

In *Clocks and More Clocks*, Mr Higgins, who is an eccentric-looking gentleman, finds a clock in his attic and wonders if it tells the right time. To test it he buys several other clocks and positions them in different rooms in the house. He then runs up and down the stairs to see if they all tell the same time and is bewildered by the fact that the attic clock is different from the clock in the hall by three minutes.

'So he went out and bought another . . .'

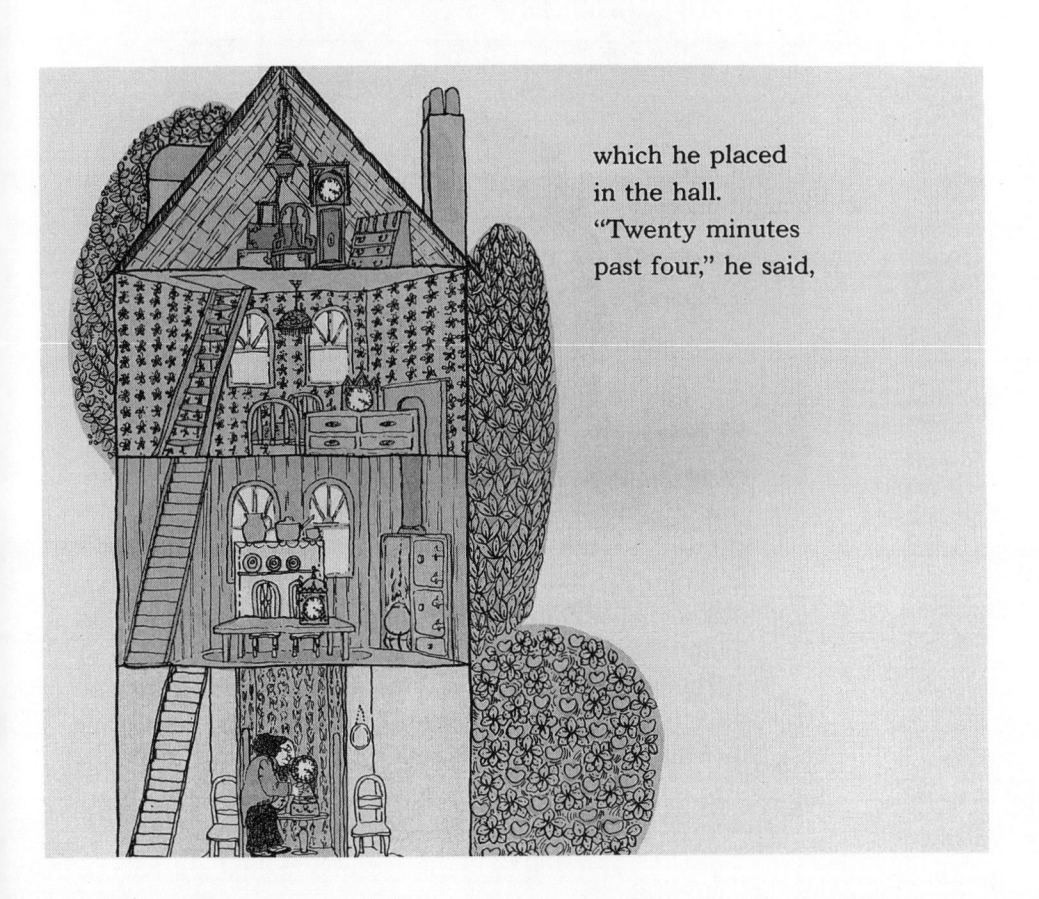

which he placed in the hall. "Twenty minutes past four," he said,

Time passes

and ran up to the attic.
The attic clock said
twenty-three minutes past four.

Where the Wild Things Are,
Maurice Sendak

In *Where the Wild Things Are,* Max had been naughty; his mother called him 'Wild Thing' and sent him to bed 'without any supper'.

That night a forest grew in his room; the walls 'became the world' and 'an ocean tumbled by with a private boat for Max ...'. '... and he sailed off through night and day ...'

PICTURE BOOKS: *Granpa*, John Burningham

and in and out of weeks
and almost over a year
to where the wild things are.

After taming the creatures, becoming their king and getting bored and lonely, he decided to sail for home 'over a year, in and out of weeks over a day and into the night of his very own room'.

Supper was waiting 'and it was still hot!'.

Granpa, John Burningham

Granpa is a most unusual picture book. It does not read like a story, but is made up of scraps of conversation between a little girl and her 'granpa'. It is important that the reader understands that 'real' time is passing (a year); but like all good writers, John Burningham doesn't *tell* us, he finds ways of *showing* us through what the little girl and her 'granpa' do together, e.g. planting seeds and ice-skating.

Time passes

When I was a boy we used to roll our wooden hoops down the street after school.

Were you once a baby as well, Granpa?

When we get to the beach can we stay there for ever?

Yes, but we must go back for our tea at four o'clock.

PICTURE BOOKS: *Granpa*, John Burningham

Tomorrow shall we go to Africa, and you can be the captain?

123

Time passes

Talking

- Talk about the different concepts of 'Time' expressed in these three extracts from picture books and discuss what young children might learn from them about time.
- Can you think of ways in which Pat Hutchins might resolve Mr Higgins' 'problem'? Check with the book later.
- Why do you think Maurice Sendak reversed the order of the words he used to describe the journey through time? Talk about the significance of the words 'and it was still hot'.
- What do we learn from the three questions in *Granpa* about the child's understanding of time?
- How do you think a young child might 'read' the picture of the empty chair?
- Can you remember:
  - learning to tell the time;
  - occasions when time seemed endless and others when it 'flew' and you wanted it to stand still;
  - 'out of time' moments, e.g. dreams, imaginative play and make-believe friends, creating a fantasy world;
  - being punished by having to spend time alone (doing time!);
  - embarrassing, annoying or sometimes amusing adults by your misunderstanding of time, e.g. when you learned that someone was middle-aged and you asked 'Were you born in the Middle Ages?' or your family had just crossed the channel and with a seven-hundred-mile car journey to go to your camp site, you asked 'Are we nearly there?' . . . and you repeated the question every half hour?

The Mark on the Beach, Jo-Anne Holmwood and Elizabeth Cross

Here is the text and three of the illustrations from a picture book called *The Mark on the Beach*.

Picture 1   Once upon a time there was an empty beach.
Picture 2   Peter came along the beach dragging a big, thick stick, then he went to have tea with his aunt.

PICTURE BOOKS: *The Mark on the Beach*, Jo-Anne Holmwood and Elizabeth Cross

Picture 3   A little girl came cartwheeling along the beach. She stared at the mark. She thought it had been made by ...
Picture 4   a clown riding a bicycle.
Picture 5   Then a souvenir-seller came along the beach. 'Who made this mark?' he wondered. He thought it was ...
Picture 6   the queen rolling a hoop.
Picture 7   Then a parachutist landed on the beach. He thought it was made by ...
Picture 8   a giant's finger writing in the sand.
Picture 9   Then a boy came swimming out of the sea. He stared at the mark. He thought it could have been ...
Picture 10   a sea-serpent.
Picture 11   Then a gardener came walking along the beach. He guessed it was made by ...
Picture 12   an elephant pushing a pram.
Picture 13   Peter came back from his tea and saw all the people arguing about the mark.
Picture 14   Then the sea crept closer and closer up the beach. When it slid back, the mark had gone.
Picture 15   Once upon a time there was an empty beach ...

Time passes

Talking

Elizabeth Cross and Jo-Anne Holmwood were aged twelve years when they created this story but, like John Burningham, they have found simple ways of marking the passing of time.
- What are they?
- How could they have shown time passing in their illustrations?

Writing and drawing

Jot down any ideas to do with 'Time' which you think might make an interesting picture book. Even if you think you can't draw, you can describe what you want to put in your illustrations and ask somebody else to draw them.

Develop any *one* of the ideas which appeals to you and present it in picture book form. It takes a long time to make a book. If you get a good idea and the enthusiasm to see it through, it can be a satisfying experience. You will acquire a lot of new skills and get pleasure from sharing your work with young children. One piece of advice – keep it simple – leave the pop-ups and pull-outs to Jan Piénkowski!

Reading

Collect a wide variety of picture books. Enjoy reading them. Notice any ways in which 'Time' is referred to in the stories and in the illustrations.

Since many of you will have younger brothers and sisters and some of you will be 'baby sitters', you will have opportunities to share stories and become skilled at reading aloud.

Select one picture book and prepare it for sharing with young children. You will have to be prepared for the child who:
- wants to talk about the pictures rather than listen to the story;
- wants to read it with you and makes up more story than is printed;
- asks questions and constantly interrupts;
- adds sound effects – wind blowing, cows moo-ing, Wild Things roaring, etc.
- tells you that you have missed something out when you have tried to 'short cut' the story!

Have patience – this is how young children are encouraged to share in the reading and how they eventually learn to become readers themselves.

TIME IN VERSE
You'll See, Alan Brownjohn

They all talked about growing into,
Growing into, growing into.
They said: You will grow into it.

– But it isn't mine,
And it's not for me.
– You will grow into it,
You'll see!

– But it hangs down below my knee,
It is too long for me.
– Oh it will fit you soon,
It will fit you splendidly.

– But I will sulk, and I will say
It is too long, it is no use,
No! I will sulk, and struggle,
And refuse!

– You will grow into it,
And love it,
And besides, we decided
You should have it.

No! – But wait –
Wait a moment ... Do I see
It growing shorter at the knee?
Is it shrinking gradually?
Is it getting shorter?
Is it getting tighter?
Not loose and straggly,
Not long and baggy,
But neater and brighter,
Comfortable?

Oh now I *do* like it,
Oh now I'll go to the mirror and see

TIME IN VERSE: *You'll See*, Alan Brownjohn

How wonderful it looks on me,
Yes – there – it's ideal!
Yes, its appeal
Will be universal,
And now I curse all
Those impulses which muttered 'Refuse!'
It's really beautiful after all,
I'll wear it today, next week, next year
– No one is going to interfere,
I'll wear it as long as I choose.

And then, much later, when it wears,
And it's ready for dumping under the stairs
When it doesn't actually really fit me
Any longer, then *I'll* pass it down,
When it doesn't fit me,
And then they'll have it,
They'll *have* to have it,
They'll have to love it,
They'll see, they'll see.

They'll have to grow into it like me!

A picture book called *You'll Soon Grow Into Them, Titch* by Pat Hutchins echoes many of the feelings expressed in this poem. Look at it alongside the poem and, if possible, share the reading of it with a younger person in your school or family.

It is not only children who find 'Time' a difficult concept to understand; adults, too, spend a life-time trying to extend it, forget it, put it off, manipulate it, spend it, waste it and remember it. Therefore, it is not suprising that 'Time' has been one of the chosen themes of poets throughout the ages.

About Friends, Brian Jones

In his poem *About Friends*, Brian Jones recalls how, with the passing of time, his relationship with a friend has changed.

The good thing about friends
is not having to finish sentences.

I sat a whole summer afternoon with my friend once
on a river bank, bashing heels on the baked mud
and watching the small chunks slide into the water
and listening to them – plop plop plop.
He said 'I like the twigs when they . . . you know . . .
like that.' I said 'There's that branch . . .'
We both said 'Mmmm.' The river flowed and flowed
and there were lots of butterflies, that afternoon.

I first thought there was a sad thing about friends
when we met twenty years later.
We both talked hundreds of sentences,
taking care to finish all we said,
and explain it all very carefully,
as if we'd been discovered in places
we should not be, and were somehow ashamed.

I understood then what the river meant by flowing.

It was Long Ago, Eleanor Farjeon

In the next poem, Eleanor Farjeon looks back to her earliest memory. You may find it surprising that she remembers so vividly what appears to be a very ordinary happening.

I'll tell you, shall I, something I remember?
Something that still means a great deal to me.
It was long ago.

A dusty road in summer I remember,
A mountain, and an old house, and a tree
That stood, you know

Behind the house. An old woman I remember
In a red shawl with a grey cat on her knee
Humming under a tree.

She seemed the oldest thing I can remember,
But then perhaps I was not more than three.
It was long ago.

I dragged on the dusty road, and I remember
How the old woman looked over the fence at me
And seemed to know

How it felt to be three, and called out, I remember
'Do you like bilberries and cream for tea?'
I went under the tree

And while she hummed, and the cat purred, I remember
How she filled a saucer with berries and cream for me
So long ago,

Such berries and such cream as I remember
I never had seen before, and never see
To-day, you know.

And that is almost all I can remember,
The house, the mountain, the grey cat on her knee,
Her red shawl, and the tree,

And the taste of the berries, the feel of the sun I remember,
And the smell of everything that used to be
So long ago,

Till the heat on the road outside again I remember,
And how the long dusty road seemed to have for me
No end, you know.

That is the farthest thing I can remember.
It won't mean much to you. It does to me.
Then I grew up, you see.

Time passes

Talking and writing

- Read through all three poems again. Talk about the different concepts of time expressed in each of them.
- Re-tell any incidents in your childhood when:
  – an adult threatened you with having to do something by a certain time or else;
  – time seemed endless because you were caught up in a terrifying situation, e.g. lost in a crowd, carrying out a dare.
- Have you noticed that when friends or relatives are talking they hardly ever finish sentences? Listen in and jot down some examples.
- Can you suggest the reasons why two adults, not having seen each other for twenty years, take care to finish all their sentences?
- In the poem, *Friends*, what is the significance of the river?
- Write down all the sayings and phrases you can think of in which 'Time' is thought of as a person. Look in poetry anthologies to add to your lists.
- Write a poem or descriptive paragraph in which you present 'Time' as a person.
- Write a short conversation between 'Time', 'Life' and 'Death' – three characters in a play.

Earliest memories, not necessarily of the extraordinary or the most dramatic kind, but of ordinary events, people and feelings, can be very significant in our lives. Eleanor Farjeon chooses to write about a commonplace incident as the earliest of all her memories. What is important is that she claims to be able to recapture the feelings she experienced on that particular hot day.

Notice the conversational way in which her poem is written, as if she is remembering and speaking her thoughts aloud.

Writing

Write your own early memory poem beginning, if you wish, with the words: 'I'll tell you, shall I, something I remember?'

TIME PAST

I Remember, Dorfy

It is in stories that we find the most complicated uses of time and as readers we have to become skilled at picking up 'time clues'.

Here are four pages from *I Remember*, an autobiographical picture book by 'Dorfy'. They illustrate some of the different time devices which storytellers use. What are they?

Extract one

I Remember —   (1904-14)

In the early part of this century life was very different from what it is now; and unless you were lucky enough to have been born "well-off", times were hard. But there was plenty for children to enjoy, for all that. One treat was to sit on the front-door-step & watch for the Lamplighter —

Extract two

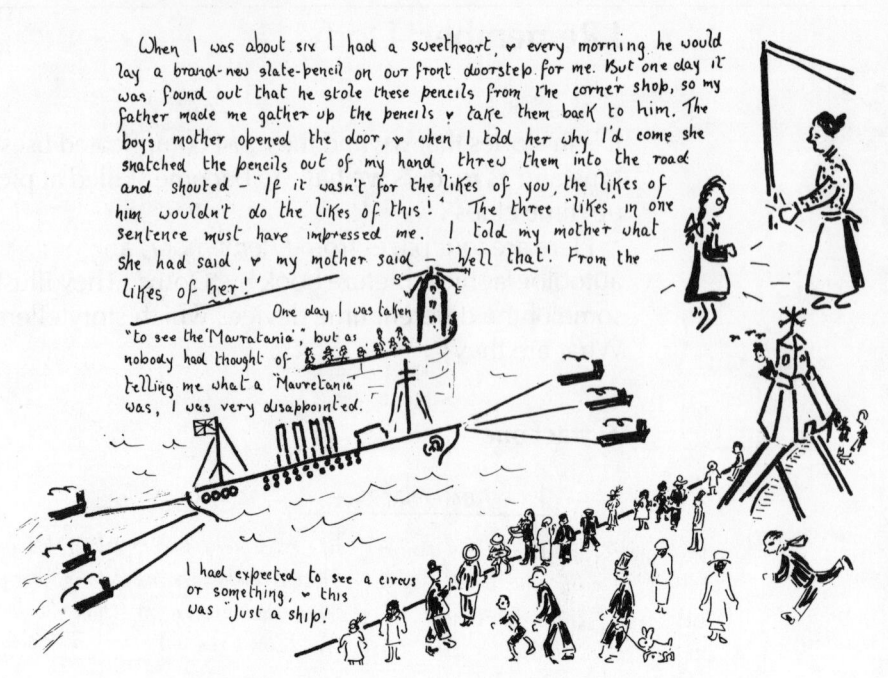

When I was about six I had a sweetheart, & every morning he would lay a brand-new slate-pencil on our front doorstep for me. But one day it was found out that he stole these pencils from the corner shop, so my father made me gather up the pencils & take them back to him. The boy's mother opened the door, & when I told her why I'd come she snatched the pencils out of my hand, threw them into the road and shouted — "If it wasn't for the likes of you, the likes of him wouldn't do the likes of this!" The three "likes" in one sentence must have impressed me. I told my mother what she had said, & my mother said — "Well that! From the likes of her!"

One day I was taken "to see the 'Mauretania'", but as nobody had thought of telling me what a 'Mauretania' was, I was very disappointed.

I had expected to see a circus or something, & this was just a ship!

Extract three

Although we were so poor I was completely unaware of it; partly, no doubt, because of the literature of the period. In the books I read — "Her Benny", "Jessica's First Prayer", "Christy's Old Organ", etc., the children were always dressed in rags & slept on a pallet of straw in the corner of a garret. They begged for crusts & always had at least one drunken parent who beat them. Nor did my parents ever complain; and they never discussed their finances — or only once. We had been visiting some better-off relations, and when we came home I asked my father why we didn't have a house with a "sitting-room", & he said he hadn't enough money for that. Shortly after, I saw a beautiful frosted-glass window; and on it, in letters of black & gold was written "Sitting Room (Free House)". I ran all the way home to tell my father I had seen a house with a sitting-room "for nothing!" When he explained it was a pub, this was a disappointment I shall never forget!

TIME PAST: *I Remember*, Dorfy

Extract four

In summer we would sometimes have a picnic on the sands. All the relations would combine & bring stacks of food — plus firewood, a kettle, teapot, crockery & a tablecloth. We would all sit round the spread. Then we would play games and have our photos taken in a group.

One hot summer's day we had a picnic like this. And when we went home after this happy August Bank Holiday the "paper boys" were running and shouting — "WAR DECLARED!" and life was never the same again.

Reading and talking

Look at the pages in turn. Notice:
- that Dorfy gives us the time span of that part of her life's story covered in this book. Mostly in stories it is left to the reader to work this out from the time clues given;
- how the writer on several occasions makes a general comment about life and then focuses on one particular aspect of it;
- that from all the things that must have happened to her during those ten years, she selects a few outstanding memories. Why do you think she remembered those so clearly?

Planning your own autobiography

It is not often necessary or possible to write at great length in school. Some forms of writing, however, need to be developed over a long period of time. Autobiography is one such form. Although you haven't lived as long as most people have when they start writing their life stories, you'll be surprised just how much has happened to you. In any

Time passes

case you will be able to extend your own 'life-time' by talking with older members of your family and by researching into the background of the place where you were born.

Writing

Begin collecting photographs, letters, diary extracts, school reports, drawings and even your first attempts at writing, ready for when you need them. Use a writer's note book for all your planning and rough jottings.

Decide what kinds of books or file you want to use for this special piece of work.

The Way to Sattin Shore, Philippa Pearce

Kate Tranter, the young heroine of this story, lives with her mother, grandmother and two older brothers. She also lives with the mystery surrounding her father's 'death' on the day she was born.

Kate experiences times of uncertainty, fear and loneliness during which she attempts to discover the truth about her past. But there are also days of great pleasure which Kate knows she will remember all her life. One such time is the day she went tobogganing on her grandmother's black tray.

Kate took the tray. It was beautifully heavy – she had never handled it before. The tray had belonged to Mrs Randall's mother, who had been in service. It had been given her from the great kitchens where she worked, when she got married. So it was older than Kate's own grandmother; and it had always stood in the same place in her grandmother's room, propped against the wall. It was never moved, never used.

Kate said: 'But suppose – suppose –' She could not think of the right disaster. Such a tray would never break or buckle; she herself would never, never mislay or lose it. 'Suppose I *chipped* the black paint?'

'Suppose you *chipped* the black paint!' repeated her

mother. She took Kate by the shoulders and stooped until they were face to face. She brought her face very close to Kate's: 'So *what?*'

Kate felt a kind of wild joy that was only partly at the prospect of tobogganing on the tray over the snow. She gave a little gasping laugh.

Mrs Tranter drew back, as if she thought she might have gone too far. She said: 'Remember, it's on *my* responsibility.' She added: 'Do you think I didn't slide on that tray when I was a little girl? Your gran let me. That's why I thought of it. Now go and get warm things on, while I get you some lunch. The car will be here any minute.'

Anorak, with packed lunch in pocket – boots – gloves – scarf – bobble hat – and she was ready! Kate dashed out to the car just after Lenny. She carried her wonderful tray.

Brian's father opened the boot of the car to put the tray in, and there was the new sledge. While Brian's father eased the tray underneath it, Kate touched the sledge. Lenny watched her. She stroked the wood of the sledge – the long sides, the cross-pieces, the bit at the front where you held on as you lay along the length of the sledge; she fingered the brand-new piece of cord tied from side to side at the front. 'Lovely!' she said of it all. 'It's lovely, Lenny!' And she knew that he liked her saying that – loved her for it. In its own way, the sledge was as magnificent as the iron tray – and Lenny and Brian had made it. It occurred to Kate – with certainty – that *she* could have made a sledge, if there had been someone to tell her how to do it, and if she had had the wood and the tools and the screws and the workshop to do it all in. She would really have needed a father, with a workshop, as Brian had. Then she could have done it.

Now they were all getting into the car. The two boys sat at the back, and Kate sat beside the driver, Brian's father. He did not talk to her, except to say when he would call back for them all.

The drive took some time, because no one dared go fast along these snowy roads into the country. But at least the snow was beginning to be well beaten down: a good many people had decided to go to Gripe's Hill today.

Brian's father stopped at the bottom of the hill long enough to unload the sledging party, and then was away again.

137

Time passes

Lenny and Brian started up the hill, dragging their sledge after them. Kate followed more slowly with her tray, which was large enough to be awkward to carry. She stared wonderingly around her as she climbed. She had been on the hill before, in summer, on a school picnic. She remembered short, dark green turf, and the heat of the sun on the picnickers, and the games they had played; but she could not remember *this*. How could she recognize something so utterly changed from what it had been? Gripe's Hill now was another place – all snow, and new and strange. Sunshine gilded the snow-surfaces in front of her, and, behind her, there followed a misshapen shadow, blue-purple on the snow, that was Kate carrying her tray.

Now, as they trudged up through the snow, other people were careering down to one side of them on toboggans or sledges of every kind. Some were home-made; some were smartly painted or varnished shop-ware. People without toboggans or sledges were using trays or anything else that would slide over compacted snow. One little boy was using the lid of his mother's twin-tub washing machine. Another child shot by on a flattened dustbin lid. Another, on a plastic dustbin bag partly stuffed with snow.

For the first time Kate wondered how she would like the experience of tobogganing – the headlong speed, the unstoppable rush of it.

Then they had reached the top of Gripe's Hill. From here opened a far view of snowbound countryside, with snowy fields and hedges and snowy houses, and the dark thread of the road with an occasional car creeping carefully along it. In the furthest distance – 'Look, there!' – Lenny pointed to what must be the estuary. Kate peered and peered, but sun on snow dazzled her, hiding from her eyes what they strained to see.

And now Lenny and Brian were preparing to try out their sledge. For the first run, they must go down together. They piled on, and pushed off, down and away. Kate watched them with misgiving.

They dragged the sledge up again, exclaiming with excitement; and Kate still stood there with her tray. Lenny suggested that she tried it out. She said she would wait.

So, this time, Lenny went down alone on the sledge, while Brian waited with Kate. Then Lenny dragged it to

TIME PAST: *The Way to Sattin Shore*, Philippa Pearce

the top again; and then Brian went down on it alone.

While Brian was bringing the sledge back, Lenny showed Kate how she must use her tray. He put it in just the right position, and made her slither on to it and sit down.

'You steer,' he said, 'by leaning your weight to one side or the other.'

'How do people stop?' asked Kate.

'You brake by sticking a heel out into the snow, or both heels. Keep well away from the huge snowball that some idiot's made halfway down. Go straight down, past it.'

Kate said quickly: 'But not yet, Lenny.'

Lenny was still too excited by his own sledging to be patient with Kate. He cried, 'Right!' and gave the back of the tray a strong push.

It started down the slope so slowly that Kate had time to exclaim: I said, *Not yet!*' and to think she might get off the tray while it was moving. Then it was moving too fast. She had to grip the sides. The tray had gathered speed and was shooting down the main sledge-way – faster – faster –

She was bracing her feet against the front rim of the tray and clutching with her hands at the side rims and feeling herself crouch forward and lean back in one contradictory motion. The air flew by her and powdered snow flickered up against her face. She was going so fast that she had no time to think of danger. She was going so fast she had no time to think of anything.

She could not think –

Air – snow – speed – speed –

She saw people streaming past her as they trudged uphill. She saw Brian, and his mouth was open as he shouted something to her.

She saw a great heap of packed snow lying to one side of the track and looming fast towards her, and her dazed mind still had in it Lenny's 'Keep well away!' – A snowball? This was a mountain!

Lenny had said, 'Lean to one side' – but she was already leaning to one side – she was veering off the track, straight for the mountain –

The mountain! –

Now!

Banged – battered – jolted – and then she had stopped. Everything had stopped, except that her body still seemed

139

to judder with the shock of impact.

Snow was in her hair and mouth and down her neck. She lay in snow; and pretty soon people began to be there and say: 'Are you all right?'

Someone said: 'My! That was a daring thing to do!'

Someone else said: 'Katy! Katy! Are you all right?' And that was Ran, who wasn't here at all, but somewhere else – surely he'd said so, hadn't he?

And Lenny was there, and Ran said: 'What a stupid thing to let her go and do!'

And Lenny said despairingly: 'But I told her NOT to!'

And all the time Ran was helping her up. 'Come *on*, Katy!' And she put her arms round his neck and he hauled her right up out of the snow where she was buried. He began beating the remaining snow off her. The other people had gone now, except for Ran and Lenny and a girl who seemed to be with Ran and who seemed familiar.

And, extraordinarily, Anna was there too; and she was saying, 'But, Cath, you came tobogganing after all! Why wouldn't you come with me, when I asked you?'

But Ran was the one who insisted: 'Say something, Kate! Are you all right, Kate? Say something!'

Kate said, with difficulty: 'Right.' And she realized that she was, too. Just bruised and breathless and very nearly speechless: that was all.

*

Chapter 5

GONE!

All her life Kate remembered that Saturday on Gripe's Hill. They went tobogganing again on Sunday, and it was good, but not quite so good.

Talking and writing

- Talk or write about any object which has been in your family for a long time. Describe it as accurately as you can, its history and your feelings about it. If you can, bring the object into school.
- In all her novels, Philippa Pearce is very much concerned with time. Within this short extract, she

TIME PAST: *The Way to Sattin Shore*, Philippa Pearce

creates for the reader the sensation of time passing *at different speeds*. Read the passage carefully, paying particular attention to the following time changes:
– The past life of the tray and Mrs Tranter in relation to it.
– Preparation for tobogganing.
– The drive to Gripe's Hill.
– The climb up the hill.
– The first run.
– Again on Sunday.

■ Make a list of all the words and phrases which the writer uses to mark the passing of time, e.g. 'now', 'while', 'for the first time'.

■ Why do you think she writes *briefly* about the drive which took a long time and very *fully* about the first run which was over very quickly?

■ How does the writer convey the sensation of speed and mounting fear and excitement in her description of Kate's first ride on the tray? Look closely at:
– selection of detail;
– choice of words;
– construction of sentences and paragraphs;
– use of dialogue;
– the way in which Philippa Pearce tells us what Kate is thinking, feeling and remembering during her first run.

■ Why do you think the first three lines of chapter five were included with this extract?

■ Imagine that you are either Kate or Lenny (Kate's brother). Write an entry for that one Saturday in your diary.

■ Write a brief description of an occasion when you remember being both excited and frightened.
   Experiment with the order of words and sentences until you are satisfied that they show your reader what you felt.

141

The Fate of Jeremy Visick, David Wiseman

I

'It's rubbish, sir.'

'What is, young Clemens?' George Williams looked with mild irritation at this member of his new class.

'History, sir. Dates and things like that.' Matthew Clemens looked at his teacher and shook his head in gentle rebuke at the dark look of annoyance that was beginning to spread over Mr Williams's face.

'Well now. So that's what you think. Who agrees with him, eh?' George Williams asked, and was not surprised to find Matthew Clemens enjoying general support. He allowed a moment of noisy acclaim for Clemens's viewpoint.

'So,' he interrupted. 'Dates and things like that – your idea of history – is rubbish. We shall see.' He stopped and looked out of the window of his classroom. His room at the corner of the building, a new comprehensive school, overlooked green fields and, beyond, the sprawling estates of the town.

'Stand up, Clemens,' Williams said quietly.

Clemens stood, a sturdy figure, brown curly hair untidily falling over a round, cheerful face. 'Yes, sir,' he said with mock humility.

'Come here,' the teacher said.

Matthew Clemens warily approached. He was not sure of Mr Williams. This was the first time the class had met him.

'Stand there. Come on, boy. I won't bite.'

Matthew drew near with exaggerated caution. The class giggled, but quietened down when Mr Williams looked hard at them.

'Look out of the window, Clemens.' Williams went back to his desk and sat there. 'Tell us what you see.'

There was silence from Matthew, a bewildered silence. 'What I see, sir?'

'What you see, Clemens. Describe to us all the things you can see.'

Matthew responded brightly. 'Mr Stevens on the rugby field with the fourth-years. Pengilly's playing up, sir. Mr

Stevens is ticking him off.'

The class giggled again.

'Beyond the field, Clemens. Look further than the end of your nose, Clemens. What's out there?'

'Houses, sir – streets, people, chimneys.'

'Chimneys, eh? What sort of chimneys?'

'All sorts, sir. A big one there, a tall chimney, and fat.'

'Describe it, Clemens.'

'It's built of stone, in three stages, sort of.'

'What is it, Clemens? Any idea?'

'The stack of an old engine house?'

'Yes?'

Matthew shook his head. He had told him all he knew. What else was there to know? He looked at Mr Williams and began to move away from the window, back to his seat.

'No,' said Williams. 'We're not finished. Does anyone know about the chimney stack?'

A hand was raised.

'Mary?'

'Pednandrea, sir. That was the name of the mine – an old tin mine.'

'Good. What else can you see. Clemens?'

'The railway, a viaduct. There's a train going over it.'

'What else?'

'Houses. A chapel or something like that.'

'It's all history out there, Clemens. Your history, my history. You and me, boy, not dates and things. You and me. That's what history is all about. How we came to be here, in the way we are, the clothes we wear.' He looked down at himself and wished he hadn't spoken. He was notorious, he knew, as the untidiest member of the staff. The class laughed at the rueful look on his face as he glanced at his baggy, old-style flannels and his out-of-date, shabby sports coat.

He laughed with them.

'Yes,' he said, anticipating Clemens's comment, as he saw from the mischievous glint in the boy's eyes. 'You're right, Clemens. My clothes are a part of history. They'd be better in a museum, I expect. But that's what history deals with, as well as dates and things. Real things. The work you do, the food you eat, the homes you build, the way you live, the way you die.'

Time passes

He had caught their interest. Clemens had quietly returned to his seat and was listening intently.

'The way you die,' repeated Williams and paused a moment. 'You live at Gwennap don't you, Clemens?'

Matthew nodded.

'Have you ever looked around the churchyard there?'

Matthew shook his head. He had no desire to go into the churchyard. It seemed to him a gloomy, forbidding place. He had walked through it once, under the avenue of yew trees; the trees had dripped with mist and the grassy mounds underfoot had been clinging wet. The tombstones stood awry and displaced, with gaps yawning between the slabs of some of the larger monuments and dark, ivy-fringed holes leading to the mysteries of the vaults below. He shuddered at the recollection of it. He shook his head again, emphatically.

'Not likely, sir,' he said.

'I want you to go there this weekend, then. Make it your special homework for me and report back to us next week. Go to the western end of the church and outside look among the tombstones until you find one to a family called Martin. Copy what you see there and report back on Tuesday, our next lesson.'

'Please, sir.' Matthew sounded uncertain.

Williams looked closely at him. 'Well, Clemens?'

Matthew hesitated. He could not admit he was scared.

'Nothing, sir,' he said.

'Right,' said Williams. 'Let's go on.'

Talking
- Discuss Mr Williams' view of history.
- What 'view of history' have you got from your school grounds or classroom window?

Writing
- Write a story in which some aspect of your local history plays an important part – it could be:
  – a place, e.g. a battlefield, a famous public house, a church, ancient ruins;
  – a monument;
  – a person;
  – an important event.
- Imagine that you have been set Matthew Clemens'

homework task. See what you can find out about the past from a close study of the records and literature in your local church and the tombstones in the churchyard. Think of interesting ways of recording your findings, e.g. photographs, brass rubbings (with permission).

The Driftway, Penelope Lively

Many storytellers, like David Wiseman, write about 'real' young people, living in the present, who come to learn more about themselves and their world by 'visiting' the past.

Penelope Lively is an important writer who is chiefly concerned with the relationship between the present and the past. She believes that each of us carries within us all the ages that we have ever been and all the ages that we may yet become – what an exciting thought!

In one of her novels, *The Driftway*, Paul and his young sister, Sandra, run away from home and the police by thumbing a lift to their grandmother's house, at Cold Higham, on a horse-drawn cart driven by Old Bill. Their route takes them along the roads from Banbury to Northampton, on the B4525.

We take up the story at the point at which Paul asks Old Bill to give them a lift.

Paul was on his feet almost before he knew what he was going to do. He took a step forward and said, 'I say – could you – could you possibly give us a lift?'

The cart creaked to a halt. The horse shifted from leg to leg, and munched the bit. The man said, 'Travelling, are you?'

'Yes. Yes, we're travelling.'

'Get up then.'

They clambered up beside him, and sat pressed together on a nest of sacks. The man shook the reins and the cart began to move. In front the horse's rump lifted and fell in a

Time passes

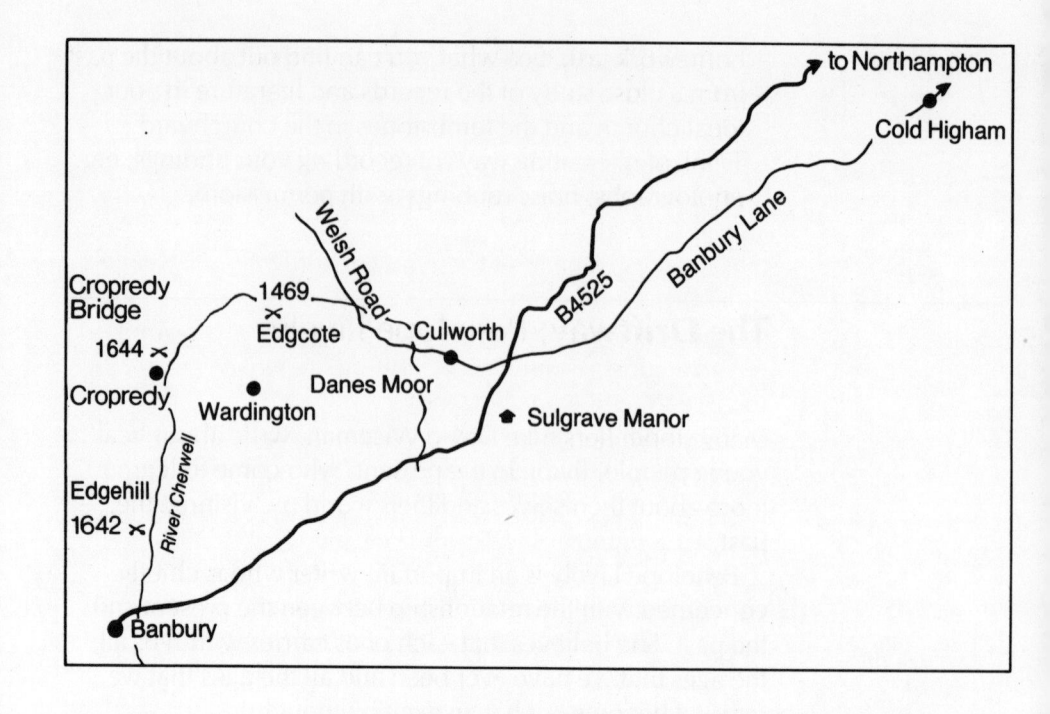

```
                                    → to Northampton
                                      • Cold Higham
                   Welsh Road              Banbury Lane
          1469                      B4525
Cropredy  ×
Bridge    Edgcote        Culworth
1644 ×     •
 •        Danes Moor
Cropredy  Wardington     ♠ Sulgrave Manor
         River Cherwell
Edgehill
1642 ×

  • Banbury
```

comfortable rhythm, the wheels creaked and groaned, the hedges crept by at a walking-pace. There was a feeling of movement in harmony with the landscape, a journeying that followed the natural lifts and twists of the road, gave time to observe a gate, a distant cottage, an unexpected glimpse of a far hill-top, with none of the frenetic rush of a car-drive. Paul felt himself begin to adopt the man's relaxed slump, his legs dangling loose over the edge of the cart.

The man said, 'It won't get you there fast, but it'll get you there so you know you've been travelling, and that's more than most can say nowadays.'

'What's the horse called?' said Sandra.

'Bessie. All brown mares is called Bessie.'

'What are the donkeys for?'

The man hitched the reins over his arm, took the pipe out of his mouth, and began to stuff it with fresh tobacco from a roll in his pocket. 'Donkey-rides for young 'uns. That's how I earns my keep, that, and sharpening knives for the ladies, and the odd bit of scrap now and then.'

Paul said, 'Do you travel about all the time, then?'

'That's right, son, they know Old Bill from Yorkshire to Cornwall, though mostly I stay around the Midlands. Up

TIME PAST: *The Driftway*, Penelope Lively

to Nottingham, maybe, and then down by Worcester and Severn, and back over to Buckingham. I like to go by the Driftways when I can: there's nothing like a Driftway when you've got animals to graze. A good, wide verge – look at this, now.' He waved his whip at the wide lane stretching ahead.

They jogged on for a few minutes in silence. Then Old Bill said, 'Going far, then?'

Questions ... Paul drew away so that his arm no longer jolted against the man's side: put up an invisible wall between them: waited for the next one.

But it did not come. Bill was looking straight ahead between the horse's ears, sucking at his pipe with enjoyment.

After a moment Paul said, 'To Cold Higham. To our Gran's.'

'Oh, ay. Well, the road'll take us through Higham right enough.' He gave Paul a quick look from sharp, sunken eyes, as though he were taking stock in some way, and shook the reins on the horse's back. She responded with an irritable twitch of the ears.

Paul said suddenly, 'We're running away.' He spread his fingers out on his knees to stop them clenching and unclenching.

Bill nodded, non-committal, in no way curious.

'We're running away from – from Christine.'

Sandra looked at him in surprise. 'I thought we were running away from the police-lady?' Paul scowled at her.

'Who's Christine, then?' said Old Bill.

'She's a person our Dad got married to. At Easter time.'

'Oh, ay. Knock you about, does she?'

'Oh, no,' said Paul, startled. 'No, nothing like that.'

'Got kids of her own?'

'No. No, she hasn't.'

'Can't be doing with them, eh?'

'No, it's not that either, really,' said Paul, lamely. Truth kept creeping in, somehow, like it or not. 'Actually I think she rather likes children.' She gets that daffy look on her face sometimes when she's putting Sandra to bed. I bet she'd try it with me, even, given half a chance. Huh.'

Old Bill slanted another look at him, tamped his pipe, and made no comment. Sandra, lulled by the movement of the cart, was leaning against Paul and looked about to fall asleep. They had reached another village – the sign said Culworth – and were passing cottages and shops once more.

Bill said, 'We're not rightly on the Northampton road, here, but old Bessie and the donkeys need water. We'll have to go down to the river.'

'Did you see that boy just now?' said Paul suddenly. 'Just before we met you. The boy on a horse. Running away from something.'

'What sort of a boy?'

Paul described him. Somehow, it was easy to talk to this man: he made no demands, left you to yourself, though the sharpness of his look could be disconcerting.

'It sounds daft,' he finished. 'But he wasn't like anything I've ever seen. It was like looking at someone through a glass window. Like he was kind of locked up in something that was happening to him.'

'Fair enough,' said Old Bill. 'He would be. It sounds to me like the road's been at its tricks again, that's all.'

'The road?'

'This road. The Driftway. This is an old road, son. Older than you or me, or the houses in the village, or the fields round about, or anything we can see now, or even think about.' He took a suck at his pipe, and tapped Bessie's flanks with his whip. 'Get up there, old lady! This is a road that was made when there was first men in these parts, trodden out by feet that had to get from one place to another, and it's been trodden ever since, year by year, winter and summer. Stands to reason it's got a few tales to tell. There's been men passing by here, and women, and children, over thousands of years, travellers. And every now and then there's someone does an extra hard bit of living, as you might call it. That'll leave a shadow on the road, won't it?'

'You mean,' said Paul cautiously, 'that it's haunted.'

'Haunted!' The old man snorted. 'Ghosties and things that go bump in the night! No, son, I'm talking about messages. Look, most living's just jogging along, isn't it? But just sometimes, in everybody's life, there's a time when a whole lot of living gets crammed into a few minutes, or an hour or two, and it may be good or bad, but it's brighter and sharper than all the rest put together. And it may be so sharp it can leave a shadow on a place – if the place is a special place – and at the right time other people can pick up that shadow. Like a message, see? Messages about being happy, or frightened or downright miserable. Messages that cut through time like it wasn't there, because they're about things that are the same for everybody, and always have been, and always will be. That's what the Driftway is: a place where people have left messages for one another.'

As the old man predicts, Paul is the sort of lad who is open to being told things and, as they journey, he meets message bearers from the past who tell him about an important event in their lives. One such encounter takes place by the bridge over the Cherwell where two Driftways meet.

They sat, nursing the hot mugs in their hands. The tea was black, sweet, and strong so that it caught the back of the throat and dried up the mouth. But it was good. Old Bill seemed to doze, slumped against a tree-stump, his chin tucked down into a scarf, the pipe in his mouth. It was very still, as though any breath of wind had been quenched by the thickening mist: there was no sound except the soft tearing noises made by the grazing animals, and no movement, even the drifting leaves lying in frozen, stiff-looking piles on grass and road. The world seemed suspended, timeless.

Something, half-seen in green shadow under a thorn bush, made Paul turn his head. A shape, an outline, an old sack flung down, perhaps, a pile of brushwood, a dog, even, huddled into the grass . . . He peered, uncertain, wary, and then the thing moved, made no sound, and it was a boy.

It was the boy who had ridden past them earlier. He crouched now under the hedge like a beaten animal. He was there, the shape of him, and the grass crushed under his weight, and the trail even of his breath in the cold air, and yet he was immeasurably far away, as though seen through a telescope. Paul, staring across the yards between them, knew that if he moved towards the boy he would never reach him: the distance between them was of a different order, awesome and mysterious. He was here, and yet so far away that to hold him was an effort of concentration, an effort to focus on that one spot of grass and shadow. And as Paul watched, motionless because somehow he could not move – it was as though he were held where he was, with the mug of tea in his hand, halfway to his lips – between him and this other boy there was speech, though Paul never once opened his mouth, and afterwards, later, he had no memory of a voice, whether it was loud or soft, or how it sounded, but only of the telling. And all through the telling, however long it took, minutes, or hours, or no time at all, it was as though he saw nothing, not the road, or the bridge, or the cart with Sandra asleep, or Old Bill, but was just an ear listening, absorbing the tale that came to him through the mist from that outline of a human form there just over the grass. This, then, was a message: a message that could beam like a light through time itself.

Cynric's story

I dreamed last night of bloody suns, not one, but many, spinning through darkness like balls of fire. And when I woke, and stepped from the hut to go about my business in the fields, the clouds to the east above the trees were rimmed with red, and the sky blazed as with fire, and I was afraid. For of all things we fear most that which we do not understand, the dark creatures of the night, and the foul fiends of moor and lake, dragons, monsters, and spirits, and the signs in the heavens which are a warning of what must come, if we knew only how to read them. And so, in all this day of terror and of weeping, I was most afraid at that moment, when the sun was barely risen, and the world silent, and the people yet asleep, and the oxen tethered, because the fear was in my mind, and not yet in my body, and I had no arms against it. Later, with my spear in my hand and death on every side, my fear was turned to rage, and rage to strength, for all men know the fury of battle, and death is with us always, and these things we understand. But now, when the slaughter is done, and the fires burned out, and the Norsemen are gone, now I am most afraid, for my people are dead, and I am alone, and I have no hearth, nor kin, and without those things I am nothing, so that it were better if I, too, lay cold by the stream there like my father and my brothers.

I am Cynric, son of Cynwulf. My father is a free man, a ceorl of Aelward's people. Our homestead and our ploughlands lie in the clearing there, above the moor and the stream: the land is good and does not flood. When things go well for us there is enough here for man and beast: barley springs from the black earth, the grass swells the cattle and turns to milk and meat, and the forest gives us fuel and timber and mast for the swine. Our people have been long here: they cleared the forest in olden times and divided up the holdings, and worked the land and made it good. Always we have had the fear of troubles: pestilence, and famine, fire, the wild beasts of the forest. But in the time of my father's father there began a greater trouble, for the Norsemen came from the sea in their long ships, and ravaged our country with fire and sword, and now they are settled in that part of our country which lies beyond Watling Street, around Northampton and beyond there, and they hold that land and take taxes from the people, and they live there according to their custom and worshipping their own gods. But in these times there is not always strife between Saxon and Dane, for the Norsemen have learned that we are grown strong in Wessex, and our burhs are many and can withstand the fury of the attacking horde, and so of late there has been peace between us, and traffic in goods and cattle, and men say even that some of the Norsemen turn to Christian worship, thinking that our God must be stronger.

But today are we forsaken, for the church lies in ashes beyond the hill, with all the huts and bothies, and the ploughs, and the women's looms, and all that we had, our fields destroyed and our cattle gone, driven off by the Norsemen.

We called upon God to help us, before the battle, but he heard us not. And there were those too who made sacrifices to the old gods, to Woden and to Thunor at the shrine in the clearing, but they too have forsaken us.

I will tell you how all this came about – this day of bloodshed and of weeping. When the sun was up my father,

Time passes

Cynwulf, told me that I must go to Culworth, where my father's brother has his holding, and fetch back from him the oxen that he borrowed from us when his plough team fell sick. For this is the springtime, when the green mist comes upon the fields and forest, and we must turn the black earth, and plant the seed, and charm the plough and light the need-fires so that our crops will be good and there will be bread enough for all. The road to Culworth goes over the ridge and through the forest, where the grey wolf slinks, and the dark spirits of the wood, but I am a man now and cannot show fear of these things, so I prepared to go on my way, but I asked that I might take the horse, that the journey should be quicker. I rode forth from the tun, leaving my mother and the other women busy at hearth and loom, and the men already gone to fields and pasture, and I rode towards the sun, through the ploughlands and over the moor and into the forest. The distance is not great, but the road is heavy from the winter rains in many places, and the forest is thick, so that from time to time the horse could move no faster than a walk, and then I watched the trees for what might come forth, but the wild beasts kept away and I saw nothing but young deer. Presently the land began to fall away and I knew that I had crossed the ridge and would soon reach the clearing and the settlement of my uncle's people, and I was glad. And then, through the thickness of the trees, I heard sounds, shouting and cries, and there came too the smell of burning, and I was afraid for I knew all was not well at the settlement, but I did not know what to expect. So I rode on the faster until I came to the edge of the clearing, and then I saw a sight that struck terror to my heart, so that I clung to the horse and shook like a woman, and wept.

There was red fire like flowers where the huts had been, and the grey sky swallowed up the smoke, and the women were running and wailing, far away on the hillside, and there were men lying on the brown earth and everywhere the Norsemen in their war dress, with their great horned helmets, and the round shields, and the shining axes flashing in the sunlight. And then I knew that they must have come like thieves in the night, silently and without warning along the road that goes to Northampton, and our people had no chance against them for they are few and

TIME PAST: *The Driftway*, Penelope Lively

weak, and I knew I must turn and go quickly back to warn my kin, and the people beyond at Wardington and at the other places, to take up their spears and prepare to defend themselves and their homes against the murdering Danes.

I rode through the forest like one possessed by a demon, with a great fear in my soul, for I had seen that the enemy were many, well-armed and horsed, and I knew they would not stay long once their evil work was done, but would ride on in search of more plunder. I rode by the outlying places crying out the fearful news to the people there, so that the men came running from the fields to drive the cattle within the tun, and to get ready their weapons and prepare to fight, and they sent a man to ride to Wardington, for there are many ceorls there, and Beornoth the thegn, who is a warrior and fought with the King against the Danes five winters ago, and was one of the King's companions.

And then I turned and rode back over the moor once again towards the homestead, with many glances backwards to see if the Norsemen were come through the forest yet, but there was silence and stillness, with only the trees spreading like a mantle over the earth as far as a man could see. And the great eye of the sun shone red above me, and I remembered my dream, and knew it had been a sign.

We lost no time in getting ready our weapons, my father and my brothers and the other men of the village, for every Saxon ceorl is used to serving with the fyrd when needs must, and keeps ready sword and spear. The cattle were driven within the enclosure, the women and children brought to the huts, and all the while the thought was in every man's mind that we were few, too few, and the Norsemen were many. And then, as the sun climbed in the sky, we heard a noise of men and horses from the west and we saw that Beornoth, and the men from Wardington, and men from the thorp too, were coming over the hill, and we understood that they meant to join with us and fight the Danes on the moor, which they must cross before they could reach the settlements, and in this way we would be stronger, and our spirits rose and for the first time we felt hope.

But when the Danes rode out of the forest we saw that their numbers were even greater than we thought. Like a river they were, a river of men flowing from the trees and along the track, and above them and beyond we could see the smoke rising where the huts still burned at Culworth, and we were seized with a great anger, and the anger gave us courage, so that our hands gripped our weapons as we waited for them, and all was silent on the moor save for the cries of the marsh birds, redshanks and plover.

We chose for our stand the piece of rising ground to the west of the stream, for you can see from there the track from the woods, and the road to the north, and the hills all around, and we waited for them to come up the slope towards us and then we fell on them with a great cry, and I saw only the bright suns of their shields as they came upon us, and heard nothing but the crash of axe and sword. The whole moor was filled with the shouting of men, and I fought among them, beside my father Cynwulf, and my brothers. I saw my brother Edric fall to the axe of a Norseman, a man so huge he seemed a giant, howling like a wolf in the rage of battle, and all around I saw my kinsmen fall, for the Vikings were many, and skilled in battle, so that as the leaders grew weary they fell back and more came up to take their places. And all the while those of us who yet escaped death were driven back and back across the moor towards the village, so that the attack we had sought to make upon them was become a retreat before their greater numbers, and while we fought on we knew in our hearts that it was useless, and the end was near.

Many times in that hour I thought I should die: many times I turned to see a Viking axe raised to cut me down, and stepped back so that the steel whistled through empty air: once I stumbled and fell so that I lay helpless on the ground, with nothing but my shield between my body and a murderous sword, but the blow fell crooked so that I rolled aside with my body bruised and shield half-crushed, but still alive. Once an axe-blow gashed my arm, so that the blood flowed, but I felt nothing, though the arm grew numb, and I could use it no more. I saw Beornoth fall, and many with him, and many Norsemen among them, till the moor, the place of silence, the place of reed and stream and wild creature, was become a field of slaughter, with men lying still under the wide sky. And at last we few who were left behind turned and fled into the forest, for we could fight no more, and the end was come, and the sky grew dark

TIME PAST: *The Driftway*, Penelope Lively

again with smoke as they burned our homes, and drove forth our cattle, and took what they wanted from us, and left the rest in ruins.

The women and children ran off into the forest, as they saw their men fall before the Danes, for it is known that in their fury they spare no living thing. They wait in grief among the trees: they, and we few who are left, old men and boys, for it was the strength of our people that fell before the Danes, the men of Edgcote, and of Wardington. Night is not far off: we must bury our dead before darkness comes, and the beasts of the forests. They are with the gods now, my father and my brothers, and I am alone in a cold world and I would that I lay with them there on the moor, with my face turned to the sky where the bright sun falls below the hill.

*

There was something hot on his knee: the tea had slopped and was trickling down his leg. Paul took a sip and put the mug down on the grass. The voice which was not a voice had stopped, and the boy was gone with it: the density which had been the shape of him against the hedge and seemed to shake or quiver, and then to recede and recede as though it travelled unimaginable distances, and then it was no longer there. And all the time of the telling had been nothing, for the tea was still scalding hot, and Old Bill in the same position, and the horse in the same place, chumping grass.

The old man stretched, sucked his pipe and took a gulp of tea. 'Time we were moving on, son.'

Talking
- What do these extracts tell you about Paul's present situation?
- Can you think of any reasons why Paul found it easy to confide in Old Bill?
- Look closely at the natural way in which Penelope Lively moves Paul from his present to the past and back again to the present.

Writing
- Jot down examples of the language used which sets the

period of history and find out the meanings of any unfamiliar words. What other details, e.g. money, dress, manners, customs, status help to give the story an historical setting?
- Choose another place on the route. Write an account of Paul's meeting with one or more characters from another period in history, e.g. a young boy soldier fleeing from another battle fought near the Driftway:
  – the Battle of Edgcote (1469) (The Wars of The Roses)
  – Edgehill (October 1642) (The Civil War)
  – Cropredy Bridge (June 6th, 1644) (The Civil War)
  or a member of the family or a servant living at Sulgrave Manor during Victorian times.
  Remember:
  – you will need to gather some information about the period of history your character lives in (see opposite for information about the Battle of Edgehill).
  – to introduce Paul first of all in the present and then to find an interesting way of moving him into the past and back again.
  Unlike Penelope Lively, you might decide that Paul actually talks with the character he meets.
- Another interesting way of crossing barriers of time and place in stories is to introduce characters from *different* books to each other.
  Describe a situation in which Twilight, from *The Dream Time* (page 212), meets Old Bill, Paul and Sandra.

TIME PAST: *The Driftway*, Penelope Lively

PRINCE RUPERT

In October 1642, two English armies faced each other at Edgehill in Warwickshire. One army was led by King Charles I. His men were called royalists or cavaliers. The word cavalier means 'horseman'. The other army, led by the Earl of Essex, was fighting for Parliament against the King. The Earl of Essex's men were called 'roundheads' by their enemies. This was a rude nickname and did not mean that they all had short hair.

With the royal army was the King's nephew, Prince Rupert. He was very young but he was a fine soldier. Rupert had gone to war when he was 13 years old. This was because his father's Kingdom of Bohemia (now part of Czechoslovakia) had been attacked. Now he had come to England to fight for his uncle.

There had not been much fighting so far but men were already frightened of Rupert. It was said that he could ride faster than the wind and that bullets could not hurt him. Even his little white dog called Boy which ran alongside his horse was said to be magic. Boy was a sergeant-major in the royal army!

GHOSTS OF EDGEHILL

Back at Edgehill the foot-soldiers of each side began to fight fiercely. The roundheads pushed forward and tried to capture the King's standard (personal flag). The flag was defended by the King's Life Guard led by Sir Edmund Verney. In the end Verney was killed and the flag taken. One of his hands was cut off and stayed fixed to the pole. Later, a cavalier named John Smith charged a group of roundhead horsemen who were carrying the flag away. Smith killed one man and took the standard back to the royal camp.

Rupert began the battle with a charge which smashed through the roundhead lines. Some roundheads ran for nearly nine miles. Rupert's horsemen chased them across country as though out hunting! A few royalists even thought the battle was over and went home. Rupert tried to stop his men but they could not hear his shouts.

Fighting went on until both sides were tired out and short of bullets and cannonballs. The night was bitterly cold. Today Edgehill has woods on its top but there were very few trees then. The soldiers could hardly find any sticks to light fires. One man covered himself with a dead body to keep warm. Within a few weeks of the battle local shepherds were telling tales of ghostly horsemen, of dying groans and the clash of swords. Such stories have been told about Edgehill ever since.

Edgehill was the first big battle of the English Civil War. If Charles had won he might have captured London. This could have ended the war. London was England's richest city and Parliament met there.

Time passes

Reading and writing

As well as the time that it takes to read a story, every book has within it many different time scales.

Take on the role of a detective and pick up the time 'clues' in the story you are reading at the moment.

Here is one way of recording the information.

Time Passes in *The Driftway*

Time and place	Events	Time clues
One Saturday morning in October – a shop in Banbury.	Paul and Sandra shopping – accused of shop-lifting – they run away. Paul decides they should go to his Grandmother's house at Cold Higham.	
Later on – same morning – the Northampton Road, Banbury.	A toy salesman gives them a lift to Thorpe Mandeville. When he stops to buy cigarettes Paul and Sandra run away because Paul believes they are being followed by a Police car.	'It was October, with the air still warm from a sun shining like a copper penny deep in the haze ...' Afternoon. 'Thorpe Mandeville slept in the afternoon sun.'
Afternoon – same day – between Thorpe Mandeville and Culworth.	Paul and Sandra walk along road towards Culworth still on their way to Cold Higham. Paul 'sees' the boy on the horse.	
Later on – same afternoon.	Children meet 'Old Bill' and hitch a lift on his cart.	'... the sun hung lower in the sky now and the fields were pitted with shadow' – and then, a few miles later – '... a flock of rooks swung across the golden sky'.

TIME PAST: *The Driftway*, Penelope Lively

Time and place	*Events*	*Time clues*
Late afternoon by the bridge over the Cherwell, where two Driftways meet.	Old Bill unhitches Bessie and the donkeys and lets them graze and drink. He makes mugs of tea for them all.	'The sunlight still poured down on shining stubble and bright brown earth'.
Tenth-century Culworth.	The first 'message' – Cynric – Son of Cynwulf (the boy on the horse) tells his story.	The telling of the tale '... however long it took, minutes, or hours, or no time at all ...'. '... a message that could beam like a light through time itself'.
Early evening by the bridge at Culworth.	Old Bill tells Paul that it is time they were moving on.	'... all the time of the telling had been nothing, for the tea was still scalding hot'.

There is yet another kind of book 'time' – that is the time that a story lives on in the mind of the reader.

Talking

Talk about the stories you remember listening to or reading which have made a lasting impression upon you.

Drama

Props and costume

- Working in groups, choose only one prop, e.g. a photograph, coin, piece of jewellery, crown or cloak. Improvise a scene or scenes in which the chosen prop or piece of costume links the present with the past. You will need to think about 'roles' for each member of your group and effective ways of moving back in time.
- Choose a 'prop' or piece of furniture as a *symbol* to represent time passing as John Burningham uses the empty chair in *Granpa*. Improvise your scene.
- Imagine that you have borrowed a precious object, taken it to school and have lost or damaged it. Act out the scene which follows the discovery of the missing object.

Time passes

Flashback A photograph or news item from a magazine or newspaper makes a good starting point for a piece of improvisation. You could begin by creating a 'still picture' which captures the event in the present and then improvise the story behind the picture or news item.

Dream sequence Everyone in the group is invited to describe a dream or nightmare.

Choose one for the whole group to act out. The person whose dream is chosen should be given the opportunity to direct the action. Dream-time is sometimes presented in 'slow-motion' movements. Tape-recorded music, sound effects and simple lighting might also be used to create a dream world.

Situation drama Choose any one of the following situations as a starting point or ending for your improvisation.
- A waiting room in which a few characters show, through their actions and possibly words, their thoughts and feelings about waiting and what they are waiting for.
- One of your group is the medium through which a person from the past or future time sends a message to the rest of the group in the present. Decide where you are, who you are and what you are doing before the 'message' is given to you.

  Only the 'medium' knows the message and s/he must decide when to deliver it.
- Use one of the following phrases at some important point in your improvisation:
  - 'That was a time I shall never forget.'
  - 'The choice is yours; it's time you made up your mind.'
  - 'You can take the matter further, but you'll be wasting your time.'
  - 'That's all I ask – just make sure that it's finished on time.'
  - 'Just take your time – there's no need to hurry.'

  Decide on the situation, the roles of each person in the group and who is actually going to say the words. The person chosen should decide *when* to say them.

5 Focus on dialogue

PICTURE BOOKS

It's Your Turn, Roger, Susanna Gretz

First look at the dialogue in *It's Your Turn, Roger* on pages 162–3. 'In all the flats in Roger's house, it's nearly supper time.'...

Young children are used to hearing scraps of conversation being spoken all around them; in play they talk to toys, often imitating adult voices as they do so. Before they can read for themselves, they are ready to understand how dialogue works in picture books like *It's Your Turn, Roger*.

Reading and talking
- Talk about how you would share the beginning of this picture book with:
  - a child who could not yet read;
  - a child who could already read.
- What do you think a young child might enjoy about this particular way of beginning a story?
- In only two double pages, what has the writer managed to do through the skilful use of dialogue?

"Roger, it's your turn to set the table."

That's his sister calling.

"I see you, Roger!"

That's his little brother.

"Roger, you know we all take turns at helping."

That's Roger's dad.

"... and that's final!"

That's Roger's mum.

Roger, it's *your turn*.

That's Roger's uncle.

ROGER!
You heard what Uncle Tim said. I don't want to hear another word about it...

"OK, OK," moans Roger.

Focus on dialogue

Twin Talk, Peter C. Heaslip

In *Twin Talk,* the author has introduced dialogue in an unusual and interesting way:

Imran and Qadir are twins.

They look the same and they sleep in the same bed.

And sometimes they play tricks on each other.

"I have a plan," said Imran.

"Tomorrow is Saturday and I'm going to speak Urdu all day."

"If you speak Urdu I'll speak English," said Qadir.

In the morning their mum came in to wake them up and to give them their clean shirts.

"It's time to get up," she said.

"Good morning," said Qadir.

"Salām alakum," said Imran.

Talking and writing Many young children can speak and read two languages. Write a simple story about one day in which two young children decide to speak each in a different language. Use your own first language to tell the story and introduce the other language as part of the dialogue, as in *Twin Talk.*

SHORT STORY

William's Version, Jan Mark

William and Granny were left to entertain each other for an hour while William's mother went to the clinic.

'Sing to me,' said William.

'Granny's too old to sing,' said Granny.

'I'll sing to you, then,' said William. William only knew one song. He had forgotten the words and the tune, but he sang it several times, anyway.

'Shall we do something else now?' said Granny.

'Tell me a story,' said William. 'Tell me about the wolf.'

'Red Riding Hood?'

'No, not *that* wolf, the other wolf.'

'Peter and the wolf?' said Granny.

'Mummy's going to have a baby,' said William.

'I know,' said Granny.

William looked suspicious.

'How do you know?'

'Well . . . she told me. And it shows, doesn't it?'

'The lady down the road had a baby. It looks like a pig,' said William. He counted on his fingers. 'Three babies looks like three pigs.'

'Ah,' said Granny. 'Once upon a time there were three little pigs. Their names were –'

'They didn't have names,' said William.

'Yes they did. The first pig was called –'

'Pigs don't have names.'

'Some do. These pigs had names.'

'No they didn't.' William slid off Granny's lap and went to open the corner cupboard by the fireplace. Old magazines cascaded out as old magazines do when they have been flung into a cupboard and the door slammed shut. He rooted among them until he found a little book covered with brown paper, climbed into the cupboard, opened the book, closed it and climbed out again. 'They didn't have names,' he said.

'I didn't know you could read,' said Granny, properly impressed.

'C – A – T, wheelbarrow,' said William.

165

'Is that the book Mummy reads to you out of?'

'It's my book,' said William.

'But it's the one Mummy reads?'

'If she says please,' said William.

'Well, that's Mummy's story, then. My pigs have names.'

'They're the wrong pigs.' William was not open to negotiation. 'I don't want them in this story.'

'Can't we have different pigs this time?'

'No. They won't know what to do.'

'Once upon a time,' said Granny, 'there were three little pigs who lived with their mother.'

'Their mother was dead,' said William.

'Oh, I'm sure she wasn't,' said Granny.

'She was dead. You make bacon out of dead pigs. She got eaten for breakfast and they threw the rind out for the birds.'

'So the three little pigs had to find homes for themselves.'

'No.' William consulted his book. 'They had to build little houses.'

'I'm just coming to that.'

'You said they had to *find* homes. They didn't *find* them.'

'The first little pig walked along for a bit until he met a man with a load of hay.'

'It was a lady.'

'A lady with a load of hay?'

'NO! It was a lady-pig. You said *he*.'

'I thought all the pigs were little boy-pigs,' said Granny.

'It says lady-pig here,' said William. 'It says the lady-pig went for a walk and met a man with a load of hay.'

'So the lady-pig,' said Granny, 'said to the man, "May I have some of that hay to build a house?" and the man said, "Yes." Is that right?'

'Yes,' said William. 'You know that baby?'

'What baby?'

'The one Mummy's going to have. Will that baby have shoes on when it comes out?'

'I don't think so,' said Granny.

'It will have cold feet,' said William.

'Oh no,' said Granny. 'Mummy will wrap it up in a soft shawl, all snug.'

'I don't *mind* if it has cold feet,' William explained. 'Go on about the lady-pig.'

'So the little lady-pig took the hay and built a little house. Soon the wolf came along and the wolf said –'

'You didn't tell where the wolf lived.'

'I don't know where the wolf lived.'

'15 Tennyson Avenue, next to the bomb-site,' said William.

'I bet it doesn't say that in the book,' said Granny, with spirit.

'Yes it does.'

'Let me see, then.'

William folded himself up with his back to Granny, and pushed the book up under his pullover.

'*I* don't think it says that in the book,' said Granny.

'It's in ever so small words,' said William.

'So the wolf said, "Little pig, little pig, let me come in," and the little pig answered, "No". So the wolf said, "Then I'll huff and I'll puff and I'll blow your house down," and he huffed and he puffed and he blew the house down, and the little pig ran away.'

'He ate the little pig,' said William.

'No, no,' said Granny. 'The little pig ran away.'

'He ate the little pig. He ate her in a sandwich.'

'All right, he ate the little pig in a sandwich. So the second little pig –'

'You didn't tell about the tricycle.'

'What about the tricycle?'

'The wolf got on his tricycle and went to the bread shop to buy some bread. To make the sandwich,' William explained, patiently.

'Oh well, the wolf got on his tricycle and went to the bread shop to buy some bread. And he went to the grocer's to buy some butter.' This innovation did not go down well.

'He already had some butter in the cupboard,' said William.

'So then the second little pig went for a walk and met a man with a load of wood, and the little pig said to the man, "May I have some of that wood to build a house?" and the man said, "Yes."'

'He didn't say please.'

'"Please may I have some of that wood to build a house?"'

'It was sticks.'

'Sticks *are* wood.'

William took out his book and turned the pages. 'That's right,' he said.

'Why don't you tell the story?' said Granny.

'I can't remember it,' said William.

'You could read it out of your book.'

'I've lost it,' said William, clutching his pullover. 'Look, do you know who this is?' He pulled a green angora scarf from under the sofa.

'No, who is it?' said Granny, glad of the diversion.

'This is Doctor Snake.' He made the scarf wriggle across the carpet.

'Why is he a doctor?'

'Because he is all furry,' said William. He wrapped the doctor round his neck and sat sucking the loose end. 'Go on about the wolf.'

'So the little pig built a house of sticks and along came the wolf – on his tricycle?'

'He came by bus. He didn't have any money for a ticket so he ate up the conductor.'

'That wasn't very nice of him,' said Granny.

'No,' said William. 'It wasn't *very* nice.'

'And the wolf said, "Little pig, little pig, let me come in," and the little pig said, "No," and the wolf said, "Then I'll huff and I'll puff and I'll blow your house down," so he huffed and he puffed and he blew the house down. And then what did he do?' Granny asked, cautiously.

William was silent.

'Did he eat the second little pig?'

'Yes.'

'How did he eat this little pig?' said Granny, prepared for more pig sandwiches or possibly pig on toast.

'With his mouth,' said William.

'Now the third little pig went for a walk and met a man with a load of bricks. And the little pig said, "*Please* may I have some of those bricks to build a house?" and the man said, "Yes." So the little pig took the bricks and built a house.'

'He built it on the bomb-site.'

'Next door to the wolf?' said Granny. 'That was very silly of him.'

SHORT STORY: *William's Version*, Jan Mark

'There wasn't anywhere else,' said William. 'All the roads were full up.'

'The wolf didn't have to come by bus or tricycle this time, then, did he?' said Granny, grown cunning.

'Yes.' William took out the book and peered in, secretively. 'He was playing in the cemetery. He had to get another bus.'

'And did he eat the conductor this time?'

'No. A nice man gave him some money, so he bought a ticket.'

'I'm glad to hear it,' said Granny.

'He ate the nice man,' said William.

'So the wolf got off the bus and went up to the little pig's house, and he said, "Little pig, little pig, let me come in," and the little pig said, "No," and then the wolf said, "I'll huff and I'll puff and I'll blow your house down," and he huffed and he puffed and he huffed and he puffed but he couldn't blow the house down because it was made of bricks.'

'He couldn't blow it down,' said William, 'because it was stuck to the ground.'

'Well, anyway, the wolf got very cross then, and he climbed on the roof and shouted down the chimney, "I'm coming to get you!" but the little pig just laughed and put a big saucepan of water on the fire.'

'He put it on the gas stove.'

'He put it on the *fire*,' said Granny, speaking very rapidly, 'and the wolf fell down the chimney and into the pan of water and was boiled and the little pig ate him for supper.'

William threw himself full length on the carpet and screamed.

'He didn't! He didn't! *He didn't!* He didn't eat the wolf.'

Granny picked him up, all stiff and kicking, and sat him on her lap.

'Did I get it wrong again, love? Don't cry. Tell me what really happened.'

William wept, and wiped his nose on Doctor Snake.

'The little pig put the saucepan on the gas stove and the wolf got down the chimney and put the little pig in the saucepan and boiled him. He had him for tea, with chips,' said William.

'Oh,' said Granny. 'I've got it all wrong, haven't I? Can I

Focus on dialogue

see the book, then I shall know, next time.'

William took the book from under his pullover. Granny opened it and read, *First Aid for Beginners: a Practical Handbook.*

'I see,' said Granny. 'I don't think I can read this. I left my glasses at home. You tell Gran how it ends.'

William turned to the last page which showed a prostrate man with his leg in a splint; *compound fracture of the femur.*

'Then the wolf washed up and got on his tricycle and went to see his Granny, and his Granny opened the door and said, "Hello, William." '

'I thought it was the wolf.'

'It was. It was the wolf. His name was William Wolf,' said William.

'What a nice story,' said Granny. 'You tell it much better than I do.'

'I can see up your nose,' said William. 'It's all whiskery.'

Reading and talking

■ After you have read the story through once, read it again in pairs, picking out the conversation.

You may have to include some of the longer pieces of narrative to make sense of the dialogue. Don't include 'said Granny', 'said William.'

Try to make the characters come alive in your reading by:

— changing the *tone* of your voice to show all the different moods felt by both Granny and William. (Don't fall into the trap of giving Granny a quavering voice and William a babyish one!);

— pausing at appropriate places in their conversation, e.g. 'William was silent';

— speeding up the conversation, almost interrupting each other as people do in 'real' life, e.g.

'Once upon a time there were three little pigs. Their names were —'

'They didn't have names,' said William

'Yes they did. The first pig was called —'

'Pigs don't have names.'

'Some do. These pigs had names.'

'No they didn't.

■ Tell each other about any amusing experiences you have

had with very young children.

Before beginning you may wish to give yourself time to think about how you are going to tell your story so as to bring out the humour.

Very few short stories contain as much dialogue as this one. In fact, it is very difficult to write conversation that is interesting, sounds convincing and does not hold up the story.

Talking and writing

- Talk about why you think Jan Mark decided to tell her story through the conversation between William and Granny.
- What do you learn about William from what he says and the way in which he says it?
- What kind of person is Granny? Do you approve of the way in which she handles William and his anxieties?

  Can you find any examples in the story when she is obviously hiding what she is really feeling?

  Why do you think she decided to pretend to believe that William could read?
- Jan Mark uses dialogue to express the tension that is building up between William and Granny; she also uses dialogue to relieve the tension through the use of humour. Jot down some examples of both.
- Write a very short piece of dialogue between an older brother/sister and a younger sister/brother.

  Find a simple, direct way of introducing your two characters, where they are and what they are doing – Jan Mark uses only one short sentence!

  Share your writing in pairs. If you have punctuated your dialogue accurately, there should be no doubt about which person is speaking.

Focus on dialogue

NOVEL

Janey, Bernard Ashley

'Janey? What you doin' after school?'

Janey gripped hard with her feet and her free hand. 'Eh?' The top of the ropes was a funny old place for a chat. But then Mary Richards was a funny old friend. Always making some plans. She'd stop at her own wedding, halfway down the church, and fix up where she was going to meet you after the honeymoon. She always had to know the arrangements, did Mary.

'Robbing a bank. Can't come out.'

Janey made the finishing shape they'd been told to: Mary did the same: white and black, reaching for the gym ceiling.

'That's good, girls. Janey, a bit more pride.'

Janey stuck her nose in the air.

'Only I forgot to tell you. My mum's out. We can go in the front room.'

Janey shifted her hold. So what? Her mum had been out two years: she could go to the moon for all anyone cared.

'What about tomorrow, then?'

'Yeah, if you like.' Janey went down; left Mary up there. It was rotten, she liked going home with Mary; but after school she'd got to go out with Lou. It was one of those things you couldn't get out of. No way. She stood to attention. When he'd made his mind up to something there wasn't any saying no to Lou. Shame! You had a good meal at Mary's. And a good laugh. It was what helped keep her going sometimes.

But she definitely had to go with Lou and that was all there was to it. No good moaning. That never did the least bit of good.

This is the way in which Bernard Ashley introduces us to Janey, the heroine of his recent book.

It is, in fact, a conversation which appears *before* the first chapter begins and might easily be overlooked by the reader anxious to start chapter one, which begins with the dramatic paragraph:

NOVEL: *Janey*, Bernard Ashley

'The car drove slowly past the house they were going to rob and pulled into the kerb twenty metres or so further on. Janey twisted in her seat.'

Reading and talking

■ Re-read the extract and the first paragraph of the novel.
■ What clues are there in Janey's conversation with Mary and the thoughts going on in Janey's own head which:
  – immediately give a clear picture of the characters;
  – show the relationship between the two girls;
  – reveal any differences between them and show their feelings;
  – tell us where the characters are and what they are doing;
  – help the reader to know exactly who is speaking;
  – both prepare and surprise the reader when he/she begins chapter one?

In long stories you will find that dialogue is used *in a variety of ways and for different purposes*. As readers, we need to become skilled at picking up clues from the conversation which usually help towards a deeper understanding of the plot, the characters, their relationship to each other and their changing attitudes as the story develops.

But it is important to remember that, as in real life, people don't say everything that they are thinking and feeling, in some situations they say the opposite!

The second extract from the first chapter begins at the point where Janey has gained an entry into the house of the elderly woman she has been sent to rob.

The old girl had probably done what a lot of them do. Got forgetful, gone out the back way and forgot to lock the door. Or else she'd left it open on purpose, only nipped out for five minutes – because the side gate hadn't been locked, had it? Well, there was still time to do what they'd come for if they were quick. There'd better be! she thought. An evening with Lou if they went home empty-handed again didn't bear thinking about.

Janey crossed the kitchen on her toes and flattened herself against the inside door: she listened once more: and

173

with the caution of a safe-breaker she turned the knob and opened the door wide, set it back gently against the passage wall.

It was dim out there. Not that Janey minded that very much, she'd got used to moving about without daring to show a light. All she had to do now was get up the stairs and wave out of a front window. Half a minute, that'd take. Less.

She took two more tiptoes – and suddenly she froze rigid. Sticking out from the room on her right was a pair of feet in shiny slippers, all twisted and still. Someone dead, it had to be! God, she'd always dreaded this happening. It made her want to scream the house down. But in the last instant Lou's training got hold of her. Little fool! That'd bring next door running for sure! She shoved her fist in her mouth to choke on the sound instead. Just slide past the feet – and don't look at them! Get out, quick and quiet, and don't even think about what horrible thing could be lying behind that door.

She closed her eyes and flattened herself as thin as she could along the wall. All she could hear was the sound of her heart as its thumping threatened to throw her closer to the feet. Until she came level with the door . . .

'Help me! Help me, please!'

Janey stumbled. Her eyes opened but she still couldn't see beyond the edge of the door. The voice was very faint but it was clear, not frightening at all really, once it had spoken.

'There is someone there, isn't there? Is it from the church?'

Janey wanted to run, back the way she'd come, out through the kitchen and round to Lou.

'Be my angel! I'm stuck down here otherwise!'

But there was something about the voice – a ring she knew – and suddenly there was no way Janey could run. How long had her nan been down on the floor before the neighbour saw the milk and knocked a window in?

Carefully, she edged her eyes around the door and saw an old woman lying there; stuck on her side, with both her arms reaching out for an empty armchair. Her chin was down in her chest as she twisted herself awkwardly to look up at the doorway.

NOVEL: *Janey*, Bernard Ashley

'You're a little angel from heaven and you've saved my life.'

'Yeah?'

'I've been down here since I don't know when. Luvaduck, I hope I'm not showing you my drawers.'

Janey had to smile. She looked down. She was, as it happened, long, shiny things that came right down to her knees. 'Yeah, pink,' she told her.

'Then it's Friday. Pink to make the boys wink, Tuesdays and Fridays, and I know it's not Tuesday. Come on, love, give us a hand up.'

Janey took it all in, an old woman, well dressed, with a round face, grey hair, and one of those walking gadgets fallen over out of her reach.

'Just look at me. Dropped the clothes brush and tipped over. Helpless! Hours, I've been down here. I shall wet myself in a minute, then I'll feel a fool. Come on, lovie, give us a hand up.' She was struggling again, getting a bit impatient now that help was at hand.

And it was too late for Janey to go. There was no turning her back now: no pretending she hadn't seen the fix the old girl was in. Besides, doing what she had to do with Lou didn't mean she couldn't help someone who was in a state, did it?

'Hold tight, then.' Janey went into the room, stepped over the old woman, took hold of her hands and started trying to drag her over towards the armchair. Strewth! She was bigger than she'd thought.

'I know I'm a weight; two ton Tessie! But I've got no push in my legs. Ouch! Oh, you're a ... good ... girl ...'

Janey had no breath for talk. Moving the old woman was as much as she could cope with. She strained and she pulled, nearly burst a blood vessel as she dragged her arms out of their sockets to get the dead weight across the carpet.

'That's it, love, ouch, ooh, that's it ... once more ... heave away ...' And with an enormous effort Janey did it. Somehow she got the old woman close enough to the chair to grab it for herself; when, with a surprising strength in the old arms, the woman turned herself over and pulled herself up to lie sprawling sideways across the seat like an over-size catch from the sea.

'Success! Bit of purchase, that's all I needed. God bless

you. Oh, you're an angel all right, straight from heaven.'

Janey rubbed her nose with her palm. She'd been called a few things in her time, but never ever an angel, not as far as she could remember.

'You had the common sense to come in, you clever girl. Did I kick up a terrible din?'

'Yeah! I didn't know what was up. I only come for jumble, then I heard you ...'

'You saved my bacon! There! Who says there isn't someone up above looking after us?'

Janey shrugged. It had been no more than a bit of luck, really. *The Lord helps those who help themselves*, was what Lou always said, and she'd never found out any different.

Oh, God! Lou!

He'd be going bananas outside! She made a move for the door. He'd come storming in in a minute to find out what the hell she was up to.

'Gotta go,' she said. 'If you're all right, like. Only my dad'll start doing his nut.'

'Of course you must. But hang on, lovie, half a mo'. I've got no jumble, given it all to the church. But you're a good little girl, and I want to reward you ...' The woman's voice had gone thick in her throat, and Janey recognised the sound of someone suddenly feeling all choked up. Her old nan had used to get like that sometimes, when anyone talked about Grandad. The woman looked about along the mantelpiece, over at the other chairs and the sideboard, high and low. 'I know you didn't do it for the money, you did it out of kindness, but I'm going to give you a reward all the same, and I won't take no for an answer. A *good* reward, mind.' She looked at Janey and nodded, emphasising how generous she was going to be. 'If only I hadn't lost the run of my blessed purse.' She went on looking, and just for a moment Janey did, too, under the big table, alongside chairs, on the window sill, just in case the thing was handy. But it wasn't. It wasn't in the room.

'Oh, *bother*! I can't drag all over now. See, I've put it down somewhere. You'll think I didn't mean it.'

Janey shrugged as if it didn't matter: but it was a bit of bad luck, not finding it, because the old girl definitely did mean it, she could tell: and when she got outside and told Lou the job was off, a couple of notes to chuck him would

NOVEL: *Janey*. Bernard Ashley

have come in very handy: could well have saved her from a good shouting.

'Give us my walker, lovie.' The old woman pointed to the lightweight walking frame. 'I'll be right as rain in a bit, get around like one o'clock.' Janey picked the frame up and set it by her chair. 'Now you come back tomorrow and I shall have that purse, and you shall have a good reward. A *good* one. I mean that or my name's not Nora Woodcroft.'

Janey believed her. But it really was a shame she couldn't find the thing now. She shrugged again, dropped her shoulder, started to go.

'You don't live far do you?' Nora Woodcroft looked her up and down. 'Over the council estate . . . ?'

Janey narrowed her eyes, scared she'd been recognised; said nothing.

'Never mind, dear, that doesn't make any difference to me. You come back tomorrow and you shall have it . . .'

'All right.'

'Good girl. Knock at the front.'

'Yeah.' Janey felt like doing a curtsey. The old girl was sitting up in her chair like a queen now, giving orders. It was funny how quick she'd changed from being in dead trouble down on the floor.

'By the way, what's your name? I ought to know what to call you, oughtn't I?'

'Kelly.' It came quickly, without thinking.

'Kelly . . . There's a lovely Irish name. A colleen, are you?'

'Dunno.' Janey didn't know anything about that: it made her sound like a dog. But she did know you didn't give anything away to anyone, not when you were playing the game Lou was, not even to old girls who made jokes about their knickers and promised you a reward.

'Anyway, you close that door tight. Go out the front way, and I'll expect you tomorrow afternoon. There's a love.' Suddenly, the old woman looked tired. 'I think I'm going to have five minutes . . .'

Janey slid off round the door.

Nora Woodcroft smiled again. 'Bye-bye, Kelly, love. And thank you, dear . . .'

'It's O.K. See you.' And with a tight smile of her own, Janey let herself out of the front and went to face up to Lou.

Dialogue is sometimes used to introduce a character before that character actually appears in the story, as in this extract from chapter four.

Janey rang the bell, leant against the porch, and suddenly started breathing hard. She knew all about waiting at doors but this was something different – coming over all nervous at the push of a button. This sort of jitters was something new: their old 'Have you got any jumble?' routine never had her stomach going over the way it was somersaulting right now. She knew what it was, of course: she needn't have been surprised. It was *knowing* the old girl that was turning her inside out.

But now there were changes in the light through the glass again and the sound of slow steps along the hall. 'Coming! Coming!' Nora called.

With a toss of her black curls Janey tried to shake her doubts out of her mind. The door opened wide.

'Kelly, dear! You came! I knew you would, I knew you would!' The old woman leant against the wall and clapped her hands, smiling like an Away-Day advert.

'Course.' Janey smiled too: but she couldn't get her heart into it.

'Enter!' Still leaning, Nora Woodcroft made a shaky gesture. 'You can come round the back next time, none of this standing on ceremony. But today, it's the grand entrance. Now, what do you say to a cup of tea?'

'Yeah, lovely.'

'And a chocolate biscuit. Let's be wicked, eh?'

Slowly, at the old woman's pace, Janey followed Nora down the hall and into the kitchen, where the small table was already set with a crisp, clean cloth and chocolate biscuits were sloping neatly on a plate.

'Have what you want, lovie, don't make a fool of your mouth. I do like to see a good appetite.'

Janey sat with an elbow on the cloth and politely pecked at a biscuit. But it was hard to swallow down: that twisting inside was spoiling her appetite. From across the table she stared at one of the cardboard school photographs, face down on Nora's cushion. Meanwhile, the old woman steadied herself on the dresser, reached out for the back of the chair, and with a tense, determined look launched herself across the gap. 'Now then,' she said calmly, as if nothing had happened. 'See what I've got down to show you.'

She picked up the picture; and while Janey ate one biscuit, then two, Nora told her about the girl who was smiling out at them.'

'Samantha,' she said proudly, 'my Canadian granddaughter.'

So that's where she came from. Janey thought she hadn't seen her about the district. She looked a right snob, too, all teeth braces shining and so clean she had to have one layer less skin. And you could tell from the eyes she was the sort of kid who wouldn't hold your hand in Country Dancing, just grab your wrist or hang her fingers close and pretend for the teacher.

'Oh, she looks nice,' she lied.

'And she is nice, Kelly, and she is nice. She writes me a lovely letter at Christmas, all newsy about her friends and her little ways. But that's never enough, is it? If only she was nearer. I do miss seeing her growing up.'

'Yeah.' Janey knew a woman who'd missed seeing someone grow up: her own mother.

'I thought you'd like to see it, knew you'd be interested. Now, that cup of tea.'

Janey poured it. She was getting impatient. She'd better start doing some jobs, a bit of earning, she thought, or the old girl wouldn't have any reason to go for her purse; and then she'd never know where she kept her money things.

'You want me to get you some shopping?'

'Later, dear; later in the week. See, I'm all right for a bit. Don't mind what they say, I'm not totally helpless. But I tell you what you can do to help. You can wash these bits and put a mop across the floor for me. How about that? That'd do me a really good turn and you'll feel you've started, won't you?'

'Yeah, O.K.'

'I'll get right out of your way into the other room. You'll soon see where these things go.'

'Yeah. Course. Where's your mop?'

'Mop cupboard, by the back door.'

Janey looked, as casually as she could. 'O.K.' What a

stroke! She couldn't have wanted it better, coming so soon. A really good chance to be on her own and go over the kitchen! She might even find what she wanted and get away really quick. She had to face it, it wasn't going to be nice, doing what she had to: so the sooner she did it and got out, the better.

When the granddaughter and her mother, Ruth, arrive from Canada for a visit to the old lady, Bernard Ashley uses dialogue to:
- show that time has passed and its effect on the area;
- indicate Sammy's attitude;
- interest the reader in a possible meeting between Janey and Sammy and how their different backgrounds may set up conflict;
- develop the story by suggesting that there are going to be differences of opinion between Nora, her daughter and her granddaughter.

The taxi carrying Ruth and Sammy Seymore from the station turned into Delaport Road, down from the bus route. The driver looked about him as if he were entering a strange land.

'Not been down here for ages,' he called back as they passed the big houses. 'Didn't know there was so many of them left. They're offering fortunes to buy up this sort of thing, making 'em into flats.'

'Really?' said Ruth. 'Round here?'

'Yeah, big development area, this is. Give me one of these to sell and you won't find me cabbing for long . . .'

Sammy soured her face. 'What a slum,' she said. 'Real *down-town*!'

Ruth looked no happier. 'It's certainly changed a lot, even in a few years. I guess I never knew the council estate was so close.'

'Well, they've chopped the trees down, 'aven't they? Now people can see each other – as if they ever wanted to!'

Sammy shivered. 'Ugh!' she said. 'How awful!'

Further down the road, through the gap in her front hedge, Nora saw the black cab coming, fixed her eyes on the two women in the back and could hardly believe that one of them was her granddaughter. But the real eyes were for Ruth. Her Ruth. And they lit and shone as mother and daughter at last came within focusing distance of each other. Nora stood balanced by the gate and tried not to cry as the confusion of arrival spread all over the pavement – bodies, holdalls, cases, kisses. The cab driver sat tight, watching it, left the women to do it all and leant over only so far as he had to to take his fare. Ruth gave him a ten pence tip. 'You'd have had more if you'd helped with the bags,' she told him.

' 'Ow long you been away, missus? It ain't safe to leave this seat, not any more.' He looked at the house with its big stained glass window. 'But I'll give *you* a decent tip. Tell her to sell. She's sitting on a gold mine there.'

With a clatter the diesel drove off and the celebration spread itself nearer to the gate.

'Ruth!'

'Mother!'

'And Sammy!'

'Hi, Gran!'

'Well, *haven't* you grown?'

'Eats us out of existence!'

'Did you get some sleep on the plane?'

'Oh, Mother, do you ever? Cat-naps, that's all . . .'

Gradually they moved from the street and into the garden – luggage, walking frame, tired legs – all in one-step moves like pawns in a game of chess.

'Now give me your arm, Mother. Sammy can carry your appliance.'

Nora shrugged off the help.'

'Heavens, no, Ruth, I can manage on my own a treat.' And with her hands shaking at her first big test she turned the frame and started to walk the uneven garden path. She knew that two pairs of eyes were behind her, and she knew that what they were judging was not just whether she could make it to the door but whether or not she was fit to live on her own any more. All right, then! she suddenly thought. Go on and judge! I wasn't born yesterday.

Focus on dialogue

Reading and talking

- Re-read the four extracts.
- Pick out the dialogue, use the storyteller (or find another means of linking the four parts of the story) in preparation for a dramatic reading of all four extracts.
- Talk about the variety of ways in which dialogue is used and its effectiveness. How successful do you think Bernard Ashley is at writing dialogue that sounds *natural* and *appropriate* when it is spoken?

Improvisation

Improvise two scenes. In the first one, two people are discussing a third person who is not present during their conversation. The third person needs to know only the role he or she is to play, i.e. relative, pupil, neighbour, etc.

Choose one of the following situations, or make up your own:

- Two members of a family talking about a relative whom they haven't seen for some time.
- A teacher and a parent in conversation about a pupil.
- Two house-dwellers complaining about the behaviour of a new neighbour.
- Two young people are talking about how to tell an old person that they have lost the money they were given for shopping.

You should aim to make your conversation as natural as possible which means that there will be silences.

Your second scene should include the 'third' person and follow on naturally from the first.

Think of an interesting way of indicating that time has passed if you need to.

Writing

- Look at some of your recent pieces of written work in which you have used dialogue. From what you have learned about the use of dialogue in this chapter, you might wish to redraft some parts of your work and comment on the changes you make.
- Use one of your improvisations as a basis for a story. Let your dialogue flow naturally out of your narrative but make considered choices about whether to include it or not and how it can be used appropriately.

VERSE

November Story, Vernon Scannell
The Bossy Young Tree, Brian Patten

Reading and talking

- Working in pairs, spend time browsing through poetry anthologies to find poems which contain dialogue.
  Jot down the title, poet, book title and page references of four or five.
  Try to find examples which illustrate some of the following:
  – One poem in which very little dialogue is used.
  – A poem in which a great deal of dialogue is used.
  – A story poem which is written mainly through dialogue.
- Talk about how and why you think the poet has used dialogue in the poems you choose.

We have included two poems by modern poets which show different ways in which dialogue is used effectively in verse.
  In the first poem, *November Story* by Vernon Scannell, you will see that dialogue is used sparingly and very dramatically:

The evening had caught cold;
Its eyes were blurred.
It had a dripping nose
And its tongue was furred.

I sat in a warm bar
After the day's work;
November snuffled outside,
Greasing the sidewalk.

But soon I had to go
Out into the night
Where shadows prowled the alleys
Hiding from the light.

Focus on dialogue

But light shone at the corner
On the pavement where
A man had fallen over
Or been knocked down there.

His legs on the slimed concrete
Were splayed out wide;
He had been propped against a lamp-post
His head lolled to one side.

A victim of crime or accident,
An image of fear,
He remained quite motionless
As I drew near

Then a thin voice startled silence
From a doorway close by
Where an urchin hid from the wind:
'Spare a penny for the guy!'

I gave the boy some money
And hastened on.
A voice called, 'Thank you guv'nor!'
And the words upon

The wincing air seemed strange –
So hoarse and deep –
As if the guy had spoken
In his restless sleep.

The second poem, *The Bossy Young Tree* by Brian Patten, is written entirely as a conversation between the tree and the grass.

'Fallen leaves,' said the tree,
'Are merely debris.
Do ask the wind
To blow them away.'

VERSE: *November Story*, Vernon Scannell

'Before a year can pass
They will rot into me,
So don't be an ass,'
Said the grass.

'Bah!' said the tree,
'They are still debris,
So do ask the wind
To blow them away.'

'Don't be so vicious,
They are quite nutritious,
As you will soon see
When they rot into me.'

'They're keeping you warm,' said the tree,
'And you want them to stay
Because they're covering you
Like a double duvet.'

'They're keeping me damp,' said the grass,
'And I'm bound to get cramp
But I think they should stay
And rot the natural way.'

'I insist,' said the tree.
'I do not want debris
Littering the ground
In front of me.'

'It's ecologically sound
To have leaves on the ground.
With them you'll thrive,
But without won't survive.'

'Are you sure?' said the tree.
'Yes,' said the the grass.
'Then let it pass,' said the tree,
'I was being an ass.'

'Did you call?' said the wind.
'Oh no,' said the tree,
'I was merely admiring
This lovely debris.'

Focus on dialogue

Talking, writing and reading

- Spend time reading and talking about the two poems. Remember that even if you are reading poetry silently you should try to hear it in your head.
- Working in pairs or small groups, choose one of them. Make notes in preparation for a short talk to another pair or group, in which you introduce the poem and comment on the use of dialogue. Quote from the poem to illustrate the points you wish to make.

   Begin or end your talk by reading the whole poem. Here are some points to keep in mind when reading aloud:
   - Take your time.
   - Decide which words are unimportant and should hardly be sounded, e.g. words like 'an', 'the' and 'a' in the lines:

   Where an urchin hid from the wind:
   'Spare a penny for the guy!'

   - Think about which words need special attention when you say them aloud.
   - Try to continue the lines smoothly from one to another where the meaning carries over, e.g. in the lines:

   'They're keeping you warm' said the tree
   And you want them to stay
   Because they're covering you
   Like a double duvet.'

   - Remember you can vary the pace without upsetting the *rhythm* of the verse. Don't let the *metre* and *rhyme* take charge – think about the *sound* and the *sense*.

   This is metre

   (Ti tum ti tum ti tay)
    Before a year can pass

   (Ti   ti   tum titi   tee)
    They will rot into me

   (Ti tum ti ti tum)
    So don't be an ass

   (Ti   ti   tee)
    Said the grass

VERSE: *November Story*, Vernon Scannell

This is rhythm

'Before a yeàr can paṡs
They will ròt iǹto mè
So dòn't be an aṡs,'
said the graṡs.

— Be prepared to read a poem you enjoy again and again until you are satisfied with the sound of it.
- Re-tell the story of the incident in *November Story* as Vernon Scannell might have told it on his arrival home.
- If Vernon Scannell had been an artist, he might have drawn or painted the scene instead of writing a poem. What images would he have included and what would have been the focus of attention in the picture?

   What title might he have given to it? You might find time in an art lesson or at home to create your own picture out of any of the ideas in these two poems.
- In literature and particularly in poetry, some non-human things are often written about as if they were human and had human characteristics (personification). What examples can you find of this in *November Story*?
- In *The Bossy Young Tree*, Brian Patten gives the power of speech to a tree, grass and wind. Write a conversation in which there is a contest between two inanimate or two non-human living things, e.g. the North Wind and the Sun; Summer and Winter; Night and Day; Life and Death; North and South; a cat and a bird; a bird and a worm; a tortoise and a hare.

   You will need to decide whether to write your dialogue in poetry, prose or play form.
- Have you heard people talking like the tree and the grass in *The Bossy Young Tree*? Write the conversation they might have had.

DRAMA

Five Green Bottles – a play for radio, Ray Jenkins

An ordinary household. The play is set in the kitchen which is roomy and has access to the hall and living-room.

The time of the play is that period of rush between 8 o'clock and 8.45 a.m. on any weekday.

GRAMP *is reading the paper.* KEVIN *is eating his toast. The radio is blaring cheery music.* MOTHER *is in the hall – calling upstairs.*

MOTHER   David! It's eight o'clock. Are you coming down or aren't you! David!

DAVID [*Upstairs*]   All right!

MOTHER   No 'all right' about it! Do you hear me!

DAVID [*Low*]   Keep your hair on.

MOTHER [*Going up a couple of steps*]   What did you say?

DAVID   I'm combing me hair down.

MOTHER   We'll have less of your lip, my lad. And I'm not calling you again. You'll be late. And tell that Maureen as well. [*Coming down the steps*] Talk about a house of the dead.

DAVID [*Hammering on a door*]   Maureen!

MOTHER [*Shouting*]   There's no need to shout!

DAVID [*Singing*]   Maureen-O!

MOTHER   Maureen, you'll be late! [*Pause*]

DAVID   She's died in her sleep.

MOTHER   I give up.
[*She comes back into the kitchen*]
Nobody can get up in this house – you must get it from your father. If I slept half as much as you lot do there'd be nothing done –

KEVIN   The world'd fall to bits –

MOTHER   Kevin – get that telescope off the table –

KEVIN   I'm looking at tomato cells.

GRAMP   This paper's all creased!

MOTHER Don't moan, dad!

GRAMP It's like trying to read an elephant's kneecap!

MOTHER Why've you left that piece of bacon?

KEVIN It's all fat.

MOTHER You don't know what's good for you – it keeps out the cold –

KEVIN Why don't they make coats out of it then?

MOTHER That's enough. And turn that music down for heaven's sake – you can't even hear yourself think in a din like that.

KEVIN It's supposed to make you feel bright and breezy.

MOTHER You must be joking. Turn it off.
[*The radio is switched off*]
Oh! A bit of peace at last!

GRAMP Never had bacon when I went to school, never had bacon and . . . and . . . what're the other things?

KEVIN Eggs.

MOTHER Now don't go on about it, Dad.

GRAMP Aye, eggs. Never. Just bread and jam and a four-mile walk.

KEVIN Aren't you glad you came to live with us then?

MOTHER Kevin, that's enough of that! There's a lot you youngsters today have to be thankful for and a full stomach's one of them.

GRAMP Just bread and jam and a five-mile walk.

KEVIN Four, you said.

GRAMP It might've been six if you count the hills.

MOTHER There's many a starving Chinese who'd be only too glad to finish what you leave.

KEVIN Show me one.

MOTHER Kevin, how many more times!

GRAMP Where're my glasses! I can't read without my glasses.

KEVIN The cat's wearing them.

MOTHER Kevin!

GRAMP It's a plot!

MOTHER Oh I don't know. If it's not one it's the other. What've I done wrong O Lord!

GRAMP The words go up and down without them!

MOTHER [*Patiently*] Where did you have them last, dad?

GRAMP I had them just now.

MOTHER Are you sitting on them?

GRAMP Don't be daft – why should I sit on them.

MOTHER Stranger things've happened. Get up. Come on, get up.

[GRAMP *gets up. He's been sitting on them.*]
There you are. What did I say?

GRAMP Who put them there, that's what I'd like to know!

KEVIN [*Low*] The cat.

MOTHER Do you want any more tea?

KEVIN No, thanks.

GRAMP Look, they're all twisted. You've got to have a head like a corkscrew to get them on now!

MOTHER [*Calling*] David! Maureen! I won't tell you again! it's ten past eight already!

GRAMP [*Reading out the Headlines*] 'BERLIN TABLE TALKS'. [*He giggles*] Do you get it, young Kevin?

KEVIN Loud and clear.

GRAMP Berlin Table – talks!

KEVIN [*Low*] Very funny!

GRAMP What d'you say?

KEVIN [*Loud*] Very funny.

GRAMP Aye. [*Mournfully*] Nobody laughs now-a-days. That's the trouble with the world.

MOTHER What were you and David quarrelling about last night.

KEVIN Nothing.

MOTHER Nobody makes noise like that about nothing. Your dad's only got one ear and he heard it too. What was it?

KEVIN Nothing.
[*He gets up*]

DRAMA: *Five Green Bottles*, Ray Jenkins

MOTHER   Where're you going?

KEVIN   Get my books.

MOTHER   You still haven't answered my question, young man!

KEVIN   It was nothing – honest!

MOTHER   Talk about blood from a stone. And take this telescope – I've only got one pair of hands.
[*Letters come through the front door*]
There's the post.

[*A door slams upstairs*]

DAVID   I'll get them.

MOTHER   Those doors!

KEVIN   I'll get them.

MOTHER   No, let David do it – it'll be one way of getting him downstairs.

[DAVID *is cascading down stairs*]

KEVIN   It's always him.

[*The living-room door slams*]

MOTHER [*Concerned*]   I hope it's about our Maureen's job. If it's not, she'll be so cut up.

GRAMP   'RENEWED FIGHTING IN SOUTH EAST ASIA' It never stops.

MOTHER   I don't think it ever will.

GRAMP   What's that?

MOTHER   War.

GRAMP   You and the boys're always fighting –

MOTHER   That's different.

GRAMP   Same drink, smaller bottle.

[DAVID *comes slowly from the hall*]

DAVID   One for Dad ... one for Gramp. And the Pools thing.
[*Pause*]

MOTHER   Nothing for our Maureen?

DAVID   No, I looked.
[*Pause*]

191

Focus on dialogue

MOTHER　Well, let's keep our fingers crossed and hope something comes second post.

DAVID　Here you are, Gramp.

GRAMP　For me? [*Afraid*] Who's writing to me! I bet it's money they're after –

MOTHER　Well, open it up and see.

GRAMP　I'm a pensioner, not the Bank of England.

MOTHER　You've got enough to sink a battleship.

GRAMP　A punt, maybe, but not a battleship.

[*A door slams upstairs*]

MOTHER　Oh, those doors!

MAUREEN　Is that the post?

MOTHER　Yes.

MAUREEN　My letter there?

MOTHER　No, love. Nothing.

[*Pause*]

MAUREEN　Oh.

[*Pause*] Too bad.

MOTHER　It might come with the second post, love.

MAUREEN　Pigs might fly an'all!

MOTHER　Now there's no call to think like that. I don't want you to give up!

MAUREEN　Oh, I'll be all right.

[*A door slams upstairs*]

MOTHER　Those doors!!! [*Calling*] And hurry up. Poor girl. She'd set her heart on that job.

DAVID　What job?

MOTHER　If you'd pay attention to your sister for once in a while you'd know what job.

DAVID　She don't think of us!

MOTHER　Do you want an egg?

DAVID　How can you go to work on an egg – it'd crack.

MOTHER　I asked you a simple, straightforward question.

DAVID　No thanks, just cereal.

MOTHER　At last!

[*Cereal is shaken into a bowl*]
and help yourself to milk.

[*Kevin enters*]

KEVIN Where've you put my books!

DAVID [*Mouth full*] Nowhere.

KEVIN Come on –

DAVID Leave go! I haven't touched them!

KEVIN That's just the sort of dirty –

DAVID Watch it–

KEVIN Where did you put my books!

MOTHER Will you two stop it!

KEVIN He's been and –

MOTHER I mean it!
[*Silence*]
Now let's get this straight once and for all. If you two can't get up in the morning without tearing each other's hair out – then at least have some consideration for other people.

GRAMP Like hiding their glasses.

MOTHER I'm doing the talking, dad. There's others in this house besides you. And I mean it. Now, both of you, hurry up and get out of my sight before I do something I'll be sorry for.
[*She breaks an egg into a frying pan: it misses*]
Oh no! Quick, Kevin. A rag!

[KEVIN'S *chair scrapes*]

KEVIN Use this!

MOTHER [*Upset*] Oh, look at it! All over the side! That's what comes of listening to you two.

KEVIN Sorry, mum.

MOTHER It's all spoilt.
[*Pause*]

DAVID I didn't want an egg.

MOTHER It wasn't for you – it was for that Maureen.

KEVIN Do you know where my books are, mum?

MOTHER Mum, mum, mum – am I supposed to know everything?

KEVIN   No, but –

MOTHER [*Forced calm*]   If they're with the pinkish one with not many pages then they're all on the television.

DAVID   You put them there before 'Z-cars'.

KEVIN   Why don't you drop dead?

DAVID   Dad can't afford the coffin.

KEVIN   Pity.

MOTHER On your way – and call that Maureen – she'll be late sure as eggs –

KEVIN   Joke.

MOTHER What does that mean?

KEVIN   Eggs – sure as eggs.

MOTHER [*Dawing*]   Oh, very funny – get a move on!
        [KEVIN *goes into the hall*]

KEVIN   Hey – longlegs!

MAUREEN [*Upstairs*]   What?

KEVIN   It's twenty-to. If you hurry, you'll just be half-hour late.

MAUREEN I *am* hurrying.

KEVIN   Mum's gone.

MAUREEN Where?

KEVIN   Rest home. Two little blokes in white coats're dragging her screaming out the back into an ambulance.

MAUREEN Very clever.

KEVIN   It's a quarter-to.

MAUREEN It's not half-past!
        [KEVIN *comes back into the kitchen*]

KEVIN   She's alive.

MOTHER Here's your tea.

DAVID   Ta.

MOTHER Thank you, not Ta.

DAVID   [*Overdoing it*]   From the bottom of my heart – I thank you dear Mother.

MOTHER Oh, what's the use?

GRAMP   [*Shouting with wonder and excitement*]   They want me to play!

DRAMA: *Five Green Bottles*, Ray Jenkins

KEVIN   Who – England?

MOTHER   Kevin!

GRAMP   Bowls!

KEVIN   Never heard of 'em.

GRAMP   Kathy – they want me to bowl. Me!

MOTHER   When?

GRAMP   [*Awe-full*]   Tomorrow.

MOTHER   That's very nice. I'm glad. It'll mean a nice break for you, a change from just sitting around here.

GRAMP   It's an . . . honour.

MOTHER   Of course it is.

GRAMP   After all . . . I'm new to the game.

MOTHER   Dad says you're very good.

GRAMP   You know, I never thought I'd do it!

MOTHER   If you don't stop jigging up and down you won't be able to – what're you sniggering at!

KEVIN   Nothing.

GRAMP   I'll have to get ready.

MOTHER   But it's not till tomorrow!

GRAMP   [*Excited*]   What about my whites?

MOTHER   They're clean.

GRAMP   And pressed?

MOTHER   And pressed.

GRAMP   They must be . . . knife edge. And my blazer? And my cravat? And my white pullover? And my handkerchief with the works crest on?

MOTHER   They're all ready, love.

GRAMP   And my hockey cap.

MOTHER   You can't wear that! [*Pause*]

GRAMP   Right, I think I'll go and clean my shoes –

MOTHER   Dad, they're like mirrors already.

GRAMP   I must be ready. And I'll have an early night to be on the safe side.

MOTHER   [*Laughing*]   But it's still early morning.

GRAMP I'm very . . . happy, my dear.
  [*He goes out*]
DAVID [*Whispering*] He's crying!
MOTHER [*Quietly*]   It means a lot to him.
KEVIN Why?
MOTHER Just . . . because he's an old man.
  [*Pause*]
  And give that Maureen a shake, dad. [*Calling*]
  [*But the old man is singing 'Underneath the Lamplight' and doesn't hear her*]
  What're you so quiet about?
DAVID Can I have a black shirt, mum?
KEVIN Here we go.
DAVID Shut up, you!
KEVIN   Watch it!
DAVID Watch it yourself!
MOTHER You two!!
  [*Silence*]
  Why? Why do you want a black shirt?
DAVID [*Low*]   Cos . . . I want one.
MOTHER And you always get what you want.
DAVID No.
MOTHER Why then?
KEVIN Cos everybody else's got one!
MOTHER I didn't ask you.
DAVID [*Helplessly*]   Cos I . . . just want one.
MOTHER And you've got to be like everybody else, I suppose.
DAVID No.
KEVIN Yes.
DAVID No.
MOTHER Oh, stop it, both of you. I can't be bothered with that now. Off to school, you'll be late.
  [*Pause*]

DRAMA: *Five Green Bottles*, Ray Jenkins

Reading and talking

- After a first reading of the extract, talk in groups about what you have learned from the *dialogue* and the *playwright's directions* about:
  - the situation;
  - the atmosphere;
  - the characters involved and their relationship to each other.
- Why do you think Ray Jenkins gives so many instructions to the actors?
- What references are there in the script to suggest that this play was written in the 1960s?

The playwright has based his dialogue on a very 'ordinary' family situation. As you discuss the characters in preparation for a 'polished' reading, you will need to avoid 'stereotyping'.

Aim at an individual approach to each character, e.g. if you are working in five groups in the class, you might end up with five different interpretations of all the characters and their relationship to each other.

Drama presentation

Rehearse in preparation for a final presentation of the extract. Note the help the playwright gives to his cast regarding tone and pace of dialogue.

Advice to young scriptwriters

Through your reading of plays and talking about them, you will have discovered a great deal about the ways in which a playwright uses dialogue in particular to:
- introduce a situation and make characters come alive in the fewest possible words;
- set up conflict and dramatic tension – the basis of all drama.

Ray Jenkins in talking about his play *Five Green Bottles* has this to offer as advice to young playwrights:

To write dialogue well, you have to listen carefully to people when they talk. Not only do you have to listen to *what* they say – but also HOW they say it. Everybody is an individual and every individual has his or her way of expressing what they feel ... and the more you listen the more you'll be amazed at the different ways they have of saying the same things – and it is by noting the words they use that we begin to get some hints as to what kind of person they are. For example – if you say to someone – 'It's raining'– one person might reply 'yes' or 'So what'; another 'But it's good for the rhubarb'; or another, 'Aye, you need web-feet nowadays'; or another 'It's them blasted bombs they're letting off'. Even if you leave out accents – they sound different because they are different.

One of the differences between a short story and a play is that in a short story you can write down what a person is thinking or doing without that person having to talk. You can say – 'Gramp mumbled in the corner for ten minutes picking his teeth'. But in a play you have to *show* him mumbling .. and show how his picking his teeth gets in the way of the words! And suddenly, because you see or hear him *doing* this – the whole thing becomes alive. So, to make sure that what you write is alive – you have to listen carefully to *how* people speak. Two old ladies on a bus, or two policemen in a fish-bar talk differently from somebody explaining how wigwams are made on Television!

Obviously then there are plenty of different ways in which people talk. But let's take one – and illustrate it from the play. It's fairly common – and you do it yourself every day. If you listen really closely to two or three people talking – you might notice two things; one, they hardly ever finish their sentences. It seems as if when they're sure of what the other person's going to say – they butt in; even if the other person hasn't finished his sentence ... listen again:

KEVIN   Where've you put my books!
DAVID   [*Mouth full*]   Nowhere.
KEVIN   Come on –
DAVID   Leave go! I haven't touched them!
KEVIN   That's just the sort of dirty –
DAVID   Watch it –
MOTHER   Will you stop it–
KEVIN   He's been and –
MOTHER   I mean it!

The second thing is – people, besides butting in, hardly ever listen to each other . . . it's for all the world as if for most of the time, they're just waiting for the other person to stop so that they can have their say; or that they're so bound up with what they're thinking that what comes out ends up by not having much to do with what has gone on before! But, as they talk about what interests them, we get to know something about them. Listen:

MOTHER Oh! . . . a bit of peace at last!
GRAMP Never had bacon when I went to school, never had bacon and . . . what's the other things –?
KEVIN Eggs.
MOTHER Now don't go on about it, Dad.
GRAMP Aye, eggs. Never. Just bread and jam and a four-mile walk.
KEVIN Aren't you glad you came to live with us then?
MOTHER Kevin, that's enough of that! There's a lot that you youngsters today have to be grateful for and a full stomach's one of them.
GRAMP Just bread and jam and a five-mile walk.
KEVIN Four, you said.
GRAMP It might've been six if you count the hills.
MOTHER There's many a starving Chinese who'd be only too glad to finish what you leave –
KEVIN Show me one.
MOTHER Kevin, how many more times!
GRAMP Where're my glasses! I can't read without my glasses.
KEVIN The cat's wearing them.
MOTHER Kevin!
GRAMP It's a plot!

Nobody's listening to anybody – but we know who they are!
Why a play?

If you listen to people, if you're honest and trust to your own experience, you'll find out there's as much of a kick to be had out of trying to see and find out what makes people tick, what makes them alive, as there is in taking an engine or a clock to bits and putting it back together again. Let your characters start talking the way they want to talk, and my bet is you'll have a job keeping up with them and their chatter.

Focus on dialogue

Improvisation As preparation for writing, work on some of the following pieces of improvisation in groups:
- Continue the scene which might lead on from the '(*pause*)' at the end of the extract. Find an interesting way of 'ending' your improvisation.
- Create a scene in which a group of characters are talking but not really listening to each other. Your conversation should quickly establish where you are.

Writing
- Using all the clues provided in the extract, write an interesting ending to the play.
- Write several very short pieces of dialogue to show people:
  – talking without finishing their sentences and interrupting each other;
  – talking but not really listening to each other.

Set your scenes, e.g. in a café, laundrette, classroom, youth club, family on a car journey, etc. and let your 'characters start talking the way they want to talk'.

6 Experimenting with form

This chapter will look at the choices an author makes as to which *form* of writing is appropriate to what s/he wants to say.

Story poem or short story?

One form of poetry you have already met in the previous chapter is the story poem in which the poet writes about a single incident or sequence of events. It is possible that many such incidents could have been written about in short stories if the writer had chosen that form. We will look at one such poem now.

VERSE

A Dog in the Quarry, Miroslav Holub (trans. George Theiner)

The day was so bright
   that even birdcages flew open.
The breasts of lawns
   heaved with joy
and the cars on the highway
   sang the great song of asphalt.
At Lobzy a dog fell in the quarry
   and howled.
Mothers pushed their prams out of the park
   opposite
   because babies cannot sleep
   when a dog howls,
and a fat old pensioner was cursing the
   Municipality:
they let the dog fall in the quarry and then leave
   him there,
and this, if you please, has been going on since
   morning.

Experimenting with form

        Towards evening even the trees
            stopped blossoming
        and the water at the bottom of the quarry
            grew green with death.
        But still the dog howled.

        Then along came some boys
        and made a raft out of two logs
        and two planks.
        And a man left on the bank
        a briefcase . . .
        he laid aside his briefcase
        and sailed with them.

        Their way led across a green puddle
        to the island where the dog waited.
        It was a voyage like
            the discovery of America.
        a voyage like
            the quest of Theseus.
        The dog fell silent.
            the boys stood like statues
        And one of them punted with a stick,
        the waves shimmered nervously.
        tadpoles swiftly
            flickered out of the wake,
        the heavens
            stood still,
        and the man stretched out his hand.

        It was a hand
            linking
            one world with another.
            life with death.
        it was a hand
            joining everything together,
        it caught the dog by the scruff of its neck

        and then they sailed back
        to the music of
        an immense fanfare
        of the dog's yapping . . .

VERSE: *A Dog in the Quarry*, Miroslav Holub

Reading and talking

■ After you have read the poem several times (at least once aloud) talk about what changes you would need to make if you retold the rescue in the form of a short story.

Here are some points to consider in your discussion and note-making. Talk about how, in the first stanza, (lines of verse which are grouped together to form a pattern) the poet:
– uses words and images to build up a picture of a particularly fine morning;
– introduces a sudden change of atmosphere by telling us about the dog;
– shows how mothers and an old pensioner react to the dog's howling;
– manages to suggest the passing of time;
– by ending the first stanza with the words 'since morning' is able to make a natural link with the second stanza.

Writing

Write the *beginning* of a short story based on this first stanza.

Think about the following:
■ *Where to begin*. Do you want to describe the place and the kinds of things that are happening before the dog's fall, including some background to the dog itself? Jot down possible starting points. Choose the one which makes an immediate impact and encourages your reader to want to read on.
■ *How to introduce a sudden mood change*. You do not have to stay close to the poem – scraps of conversation could be used dramatically to tell us about the dog's misfortune.
■ *How to develop the reactions of the people*. Appropriate dialogue could be introduced here between one or two of the mothers, one mother and the pensioner or any other character you wish to be involved. Improvisation in pairs might help you with your writing.
■ *How to suggest the passing of time*. The dog has been in the quarry a long time.

Talking and reading

Share some of your writing. Talk about how you might *develop* your stories. Look closely at the rest of the poem and decide which parts in your story are going to be *filled*

203

Experimenting with form

out or *cut* out, e.g.
- the arrival of the boys on the scene and the decision to build the raft;
- building the raft;
- the man with the brief case; his decision to sail with them;
- the journey – note that in the poem this is seen, from the boys' point of view, as a great and perilous adventure;
- the actual rescue;
- the return journey.

Writing

Write the whole story. Keep in mind:
- the overall *shape* of your story and the incident at the centre of it;
- a balance between dialogue and description;
- the importance of making suitable links between different parts of your story;
- effective use of contrast;
- when and how to end the story.

Talking and reading

Working in pairs:
- share readings of your stories and the poem;
- talk about what you have learned about the main differences between this story poem and your short stories.

Drama

Use any of the ideas from *A Dog in the Quarry* on which to base your own improvisations.
  Here are some suggestions for work in pairs. A conversation between:
- two mothers in the park;
- one mother and the old aged pensioner;
- two boys;
- the man with the briefcase and a member of his family.

SHORT STORY

Children, Slawomir Mrozek

That winter there was plenty of snow.

In the square children were making a snowman.

The square was vast. Many people passed through it every day and the windows of many offices kept it under constant observation. The square did not mind, it just continued to stretch into the distance. In the very centre of it the children, laughing and shouting, were engaged in the making of a ridiculous figure.

First they rolled a large ball. That was the trunk. Next came a small ball – the shoulders. An even smaller ball followed – the head. Tiny pieces of coal made a row of suitable buttons running from top to bottom. The nose consisted of a carrot. In other words it was a perfectly ordinary snowman, not unlike the thousands of similar figures, which, the snow permitting, spring up across the country every year.

All this gave the children a great deal of fun. They were very happy.

Many passers-by stopped to admire the snowman and went on their way. Government offices continued to work as if nothing had happened.

The children's father was glad that they should be getting exercise in the fresh air, acquiring rosy cheeks and healthy appetites.

In the evening, when they were all at home, someone knocked at the door. It was the newsagent who had a kiosk in the square. He apologised profusely for disturbing the family so late and for troubling them, but he felt it his duty to have a few words with the father. Of course, he knew the children were still small, but that made it all the more important to keep an eye on them, in their own interest. He would not have dared to come were it not for his concern for the little ones. One could say his visit had an educational purpose. It was about the snowman's nose the children had made out of a carrot. It was a red nose. Now, he, the newsagent, also had a red nose. Frostbite, not drink, you know. Surely there would be no earthly reason for making a public allusion to the colour of his nose. He would be grateful if this did not happen again. He really had the upbringing of the children at heart.

The father was worried by this speech. Of course children could not be allowed to ridicule people, even those with red noses. They were probably still too young to understand. He called them, and, pointing at the newsagent, asked severely: 'Is it true that, with this gentleman in mind, you gave your snowman a red nose?'

The children were genuinely surprised. At first they did not see the point of the question. When they did, they answered that the thought had never crossed their minds.

Just in case, they were told to go to bed without supper.

The newsagent was grateful and made for the door. There he met face to face with the Chairman of the Co-operative. The father was delighted to greet such a distinguished person in his house.

On seeing the children, the Chairman chided: 'Ah, here are your brats. You must keep them under control, you know. Small, but already impertinent. What do you think I saw from the window of my office this afternoon? If you please, they were making a snowman.'

'If it's about its nose . . .'

'Nose, fiddlesticks! Just imagine, first they made one ball of snow, then another and yet another. And then what do you think? They put one ball on top of the other and the third on top of both of them. Isn't it exasperating?'

The father did not understand and the Chairman went on angrily: 'You don't see! But it's crystal clear what they meant. They wanted to say that in our Co-operative one thief sits on top of another. And that's libel. Even when one writes such things to the paper one has to produce some proof, and all the more so when one makes a public demonstration in the square.'

However, the Chairman was a considerate, tolerant man. He would make allowances for youth and thoughtlessness. He would not insist on a public apology. But it must not happen again.

Asked, if, when putting one snowball on top of the other, they wished to convey that in the Co-operative one thief was sitting on top of another, the children replied in the negative and burst into tears. Just in case, however, they were ordered to stand in a corner.

That was not the end of the day. Sleigh bells could be heard outside and soon two men were at the door. One of them was a fat stranger in a sheepskin coat, the other – the President of the local National Council himself.

'It's about the children,' they announced in unison from the door.

These calls were becoming a matter of routine. Both men were offered chairs. The President looked askance at the stranger, wondering who he might be, and decided to speak first.

'I'm astonished that you should tolerate subversive activities in your own family. But perhaps you are politically ignorant? If so, you'd better admit it right away.'

The father did not understand why he should be politically ignorant.

'One can see it at a glance by your children's behaviour. Who makes fun of the People's authority? Your children do. They made a snowman outside the window of my study.'

'Oh, I understand,' whispered the father, 'you mean that one thief . . .'

'Thief, my foot. But do you know the meaning of the snowman outside the window of the President of the National Council? I know very well what people are saying about me. Why don't your brats make a snowman outside Adenaurer's window, for instance? Well, why not? You don't answer. That silence speaks volumes. You'll have to take the consequences.'

On hearing the word 'consequences' the fat stranger rose and furtively tiptoed out of the room. Outside, the sleigh bells tinkled and faded into the distance.

'Yes, my dear sir,' the President said, 'you'd better reflect on all these implications. And one more thing. It's entirely my private affair that I walk about my house with my fly undone and your children have no right to make fun of it. Those buttons on the snowman, from top to bottom, that's ambiguous. And I'll tell you something: if I like, I can walk about my house without my trousers and it's none of your children's business. You'd better remember that.'

The accused summoned his children from the corner and demanded that they confess. When making the snowman had they had the President in mind and, by adorning the figure with buttons from top to bottom had they made an

Experimenting with form

additional joke, in very bad taste, alluding to the fact that the President walks about his house with his fly undone?

With tears in their eyes the children assured him that they had made the snowman just for fun, without any ulterior motive. Just in case, however, apart from being deprived of their supper and sent to the corner, they were now made to kneel on the hard floor.

That night several more people knocked at the door but they obtained no reply.

The following morning I was passing a little garden and I saw the children there. The square having been declared out of bounds the children were discussing how best to occupy themselves in the confined space.

'Let's make a snowman,' said one.

'An ordinary snowman is no fun,' said another.

'Let's make the newsagent. We'll give him a red nose, because he drinks. He said so himself last night,' said the third.

'And I want to make the Co-op.'

'And I want to make the President, silly fool. And we'll give him buttons because he walks with his fly undone.'

There was an argument but in the end the children agreed; they would make all of them in turn.

They started working with gusto.

Reading

After reading through the story individually, prepare a group presentation of it allocating parts and possibly using several narrators.

In this short story by a modern Polish writer, we see that what starts out as child-like innocent play becomes an act of rebellion.

Talking and writing

- Pick out the words and phrases which set the scene in the square stressing the happiness and the innocence of the children at play. Are there any hints that the situation might change?
- Make a list of the people in the story. Why do you think they are not given names but only introduced through their positions in the town?

Who is the fat stranger? What is his part in the story?

SHORT STORY: *Children*, Slawomir Mrozek

- Discuss the meaning of the word *satire*. What serious comments is the writer making in this humorous story? You might like to talk about any television programmes or cartoon drawings which make use of satire.

Poets throughout the ages have written satirical poems. This short story might well have been written as a story poem. Think about the changes that would need to be made if the ideas were presented in 'free verse' form as in *The Dog in the Quarry*.

Writing

Write a story poem based on the ideas in *Children* — choose your own title.

What follows is one pupil's first and second draft taken from the beginning of the story. Note and think about the differences between the two drafts. You may decide to use part or all of this to get started.

First draft

There was plenty of snow
In the square children were making a snowman
First they rolled a large ball
That was the trunk
Next came a smaller ball
That was the shoulders
An even smaller ball followed – the head
Tiny pieces of coal made a row of buttons
The nose consisted of a carrot
All this gave the children a great deal of fun
They were very happy.
Passers-by stopped to admire the snowman
Then went on their way
Government offices continued to work
To work as if nothing had happend.
The children's father was glad.
Glad that they should be getting exercise
In the fresh air, acquiring rosy cheeks and healthy appetites

In the evening when they were all at home
The newsagent from the kiosk in the square
knocked at the door.

Experimenting with form

Second draft

The Snowman in the Square
a political satire

That winter there was plenty of snow.
In the square, in the very centre of the square,
children were making a snowman.
First they rolled a large ball
That was the trunk
Next came a smaller ball
That was the shoulders,
Next an even smaller ball
That was the head.
Pieces of coal for buttons
a carrot for a nose
What a ridiculous figure!

All this gave the children a great deal of fun;
They were very happy.
Passers-by stopped to admire the snowman
But the Government offices continued to work,
To work as if nothing had happened.

The children's father was glad,
Glad that they should be in the fresh air
Getting exercise, acquiring rosy cheeks and healthy appetites.

In the evening, when they were all at home,
The newsagent from the kiosk in the square
Knocked at the door.

Short story or play script?

Many short stories, such as *Children* above, are often adapted as playscripts for radio or television. Although they may be considered to be too short for stage presentation, they provide interesting material for you to adapt for classroom drama or reading aloud. Another advantage of making a playscript from a short story that you have talked about is that you can enjoy sharing in the writing by working in pairs or small groups.

SHORT STORY: *Children*, Slawomir Mrozek

Which stories?
Not every short story will make an interesting play. Choose one which:
- you have enjoyed reading and in which the action is exciting;
- centres around a single, dramatic event;
- introduces a few interesting and varied characters;
- already contains a lot of dialogue which you will be able to use in your script;
- provides opportunities for improvisation work which will help you with your script writing.

Lay-out of playscript
- Put the speaker's name on the left-hand side of the page and underline it.
- Do not use speech marks or include words such as 'she said', 'he replied', etc.
- In brackets, write simple stage directions and instructions to the actors at appropriate points in the dialogue. It should be clear from the words how they should be spoken so don't include too many instructions.

Drama　　*Children*
Working in groups, think of this story as a play for radio. Use a narrator and sound effects to link snatches of conversations, e.g.
- children playing and talking as they build the snowman;
- people passing in the square;
- father to children;
- father to newsagent, etc.

Write down and try out your dialogues. Decide on an order and practise using a tape recorder and suitable sound effects.

Experimenting with form

NOVEL INTO PLAY

The Dream Time, Henry Treece

You will probably have seen many films, television and stage plays which started out as novels.

School drama productions are quite often based on well-known stories. On a much smaller scale, it is worthwhile looking at a novel you are studying as a group and selecting from it certain dramatic episodes which would make exciting playscripts.

Sharing your own dramatic presentation of parts of novels is one excellent way of introducing books to other groups of pupils in the school.

One short novel which adapts well into a powerful drama is *The Dream Time* by Henry Treece. It tells the story of the outcast, crippled boy, Crookleg who, because he does not want to be a fighting man, runs away from his father's tribe. He wanders in search of a peace-loving people who will allow him to carve wood and work with clay.

We take up the story as Crookleg is persuaded by Wander, headwoman of the River Folk, to become their chieftain; she renames him Twilight.

Twilight stayed with them for many months. The folk brought pieces of soft stone and copper to him and asked him to make brooches out of them. They gave him a hut to work in, down by the blue river and left offerings of food and drink and deer hides in return for the things he made.

His head was full of shapes and his hands were hardly ever still. With his knives and chisels of bone and flint, he made the shapes of stags running, eagles flying, fish swimming and men prancing into battle with their spears in their hands and their wicker shields held before them. The warriors would come and lean at his doorpost every day, watching his swift hands at their work. One of them called Adder said, 'If I could do that I would be the happiest of men. Better to make such things than to stand alone against bears and wolves. If I had a son I would hope that he could do what you do. Could you show another man how to make such things?'

Twilight shook his head. 'I do not know myself how they will turn out,' he said, 'until I have made them. It is in my head and my eyes and my hands. It is not a thing that can be told to others.'

The warriors nodded and one of them said, 'It is as I thought, it is your own magic, only for you. If you passed it on to someone else, you would lose part of it and then your things would not be so good to look at.'

For the warriors Twilight carved knife handles and made the shapes of twining snakes round their spear shafts. For Wander he made another brooch, of a black stone that a boy found by the river. It was in the shape of a man's hand holding a wheat ear. When he gave it to her she said, 'Now you can never leave us, Twilight. Now I know what you are. You are a man who can fetch the corn out of the earth so that the reapers can hold it in their hands and cut it with their sickles. It is all clear to me now that if you left us our crops would stop growing and then we should starve. I ask you once more, will you be our chief and rule the folk, sitting beside me in the council hut?'

So Twilight gave in and did as she asked. The River Folk sang and danced at this, and all in the village went about laughing at the thought that now they would never have a bad harvest again.

That year the barley came up out of the earth so thickly that a man could not put a finger between the shoots. It was the best crop the folk had ever known.

When Twilight passed along the path between the thatched houses, women came out and kneeled on the ground. Some of them asked him to touch their children when they had coughs or had broken a bone. They said that Twilight could make them well again. He did as they asked, but always told the women that his only magic was in his carving and drawing. They did not believe him, and thought that he was joking with them.

Then, when all was going well, one bright morning the boy who watched on the hill above the river came running into the village shouting that the Fish Folk were coming in their skin boats. Wander took Twilight on to the hill and pointed. 'He is right', she said. 'I have never seen so many of them. There are two bands of them and three men in each boat. It is a war band and the chief in the first boat is called Shark. He has red hair and blue eyes and carries an axe of whalebone. He is the fiercest of men. It will not be easy for our war-men to drive them away. What shall we do, Twilight?'

He bit at his knuckles thinking. Then he said, 'Who am I to tell war-men what to do, I cannot fight?'

But just then Adder came running up to them and kneeled before Twilight. 'What shall we do, master?' he said.

'There are two of them to one of us. What shall we do? You must tell us.'

Twilight said, 'If you fight they will kill us all and take the women and children away with them. If we run away they will take the village and the River Folk will never have a place to be in again. If I had to decide, I would say that we should talk to them and ask them to go back to their own place and leave us alone.'

Adder laughed behind his hand at this, but Wander nodded and said, 'If you say this, then we will do this. But they will not listen to us.'

In the village the River Folk were gathered, the women and children surrounded by a ring of war-men who were waiting with their spears stuck out.

Then the round hide-covered boats of the Fish Folk pulled in among the reeds and their war-men leaped out with their bone axes and came running. Shark led them, with white clay over his face and his hair greased and bound up on top of his head to make him look taller.

When Twilight saw him, he was very frightened. But he stood beside Wander and tried not to shiver. His face and hands were very wet as Shark came striding towards them, grinning like a sea monster, his blue eyes as sightless as flints.

So they faced one another, with only five paces between them, and were silent for a time. Then Wander said very bravely, 'What have you come for? Are there no more fish in the sea?'

Shark grinned worse than ever and said, 'There are always fish in our sea. We do not go hungry like other folk. We are a lucky folk and a brave folk. Have you not heard?'

Wander said in her firm voice, 'I have heard many things of you and not many of them are good. What have you come for?'

Shark laughed back at his clustered war-men then said, 'We have heard of the pretty things you have here. We have heard of the one who makes them and who brings luck on your village. So we have come for the pretty things and also for the man. We shall take the things and the man back with us and shall hurt no one. If you will not give them up, we shall take them just the same, but we shall do other things as well, and you will not like what we do to you and to your village.'

Then Twilight felt all the River Folk looking at him, so he spoke up at last and said, 'If you take the things away, their luck will leave them and you will bring sadness on your village. And if you take me away I shall not be able to work for you. I shall not be happy with you and so I shall forget my magic. It will be a bad bargain for all of us.'

Shark said, 'You are braver now than when we met before.' He pretended to throw his axe at Twilight, but Twilight stood his ground before all the folk and did not move. Shark looked angry at this. No one outfaced him usually. He said roughly, 'When I speak, all the folk listen. I do not like it when a crippled fellow from inland stands against me with words. I shall take the things and you also. We will test your words then. If the things bring us bad luck, we will throw them into the sea, and the bad luck will end. And if you will not work for us, then we will see that you work for no one at all, for we shall hold your hands in the fire until they are burned sticks. What have you to say to that, lame one?'

Now all the River Folk gazed at Twilight and he suddenly forgot his fear. He turned to Adder and said, 'Lend me your spear, brother. The talk is ended. Who can expect a sea monster to understand the wisdom of men?'

At first there was a heavy silence, then suddenly Shark began to laugh and all his war-men joined him, bending and slapping their thighs. Even the River Folk laughed a little, but most of them did it behind their hands.

Adder said, 'I will go in your place, Twilight. I might last a little longer against this man.'

But Twilight put on a hard face and said, 'Did you not hear me? Give me your spear. Why should you die for me? I did not ask you to.'

Adder gave him the spear and Twilight glanced round to see where there was space for him to move back when Shark rushed at him with that terrible axe.

He set himself, with one leg well behind the other, to keep his balance, then he said, 'Let us begin, if we are going to.'

Shark was still laughing and the water was running out of his pale eyes on to his brown cheeks. He stopped laughing suddenly and ran at Twilight without any warning. But Twilight had the luck to get his spear up and pointed at Shark's chest, and this stopped the rush. Shark looked at the little wound in surprise and put his left hand to it to feel how deep it was. Then he became very angry and started to yell. Twilight felt quite sorry at what he had done, but he did not have much time to feel like that because Shark had dodged round the spear and had struck out with the bone axe. Twilight saw it coming but could not step aside fast enough. Shark was so angry that he did not aim well and the slippery handle turned in his hand so that it was the flat side of the axe that hit Twilight in the ribs and not the keen edge. It knocked the breath out of him, but did not cut him. Now he was so furious that he forgot all fear and all sorrow, and before Shark could strike again, he poked the spear point at Shark's legs. Shark shouted out and began to hop round, saying what he would do in a moment. He even put his axe under his left arms so that he could bend and look at the cut in his knee. And as he did this, Adder whispered, 'Now, Twilight, now you can have him.'

Then Twilight poked out again and this time missed Shark, but knocked the axe on to the ground.

'Now, now, now!' the River Folk yelled.

But Twilight felt all the anger go out of him and he could not do it. He was suddenly shocked when Wander stepped forward and swept her foot out, knocking Shark off balance. And then Adder snatched back the spear and pushed it through the Fish chieftain into the ground.

Everyone began to scream out then, and the River Folk swarmed all over the enemy. Even the women and children hung on to arms and legs while the war-men used their spears and axes.

And when it was over, Fish Folk lay sprawled from the village gate across the barley field and right to the river reeds where their boats still waited.

Adder said laughing, 'They will not need their boats again. We shall use them. You did well today, Twilight. Now we have a war-chief among us. You did not tell us that you could fight as well as make brooches.'

Wander said, 'Go away, Adder, and see that all the Fish men are thrown into the river. It will carry them away from us. I do not want to see any more of them.'

Twilight said, 'I am so sick at what I have done I shall never take up a spear again.'

Playscript

We created the playscript on page 218 based on the extract above. Before we started we had to make certain decisions, such as:
- whether to use a narrator;
- how much dialogue to use from the story;
- whether to change the order in which the events happened in the story;
- whether characters should be added or cut out of the drama;
- what information should be given in the form of stage directions and instructions to the actors.

We tried to think of an interesting way of involving the whole class in the drama by writing 'messages in the margin'. The following symbols are used to show for whom the messages are intended, but everyone can take part in the discussion and the decision making.

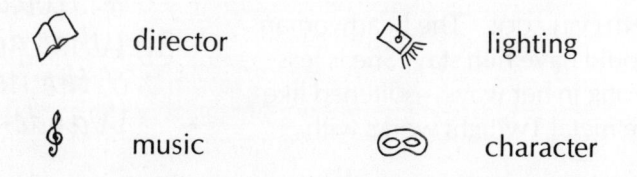

📖	director	💡	lighting
𝄞	music	∞	character

Experimenting with form

Act 3 Scene 3

One year later in **the village of the River Folk**
Villagers grouped together working and talking.

FIRST VILLAGER   In all my lifetime I have never seen the barley so thick. A man could not put a finger between the shoots.

SECOND VILLAGER   It is the best crop we have ever known.

THIRD VILLAGER   Do you believe the magic comes from the carving on the stone that Twilight gave to the headwoman?

FOURTH VILLAGER   Hush. Adder said it was in Twilight's *hands and head*, the magic, and could not be passed into the stone or carved into the wood.

FIFTH VILLAGER   There is certainly magic in his hands – healing magic. Little Stone was sick with a strong fever until Twilight touched her head. Then the hotness left her and she stopped using a strange tongue and became herself again.

SIXTH VILLAGER   He does not live easily amongst us. There is a faraway sadness in his eyes that I have seen when his knife rests in his hands.

SEVENTH VILLAGER   The headwoman would have him stay. She is less strong in her ways – softened like the metal Twilight works with.

📖 Set? Plan the most effective use of the space available taking into consideration the following groupings:
(a) villagers
(b) Twilight and Wander
(c) Boy Watcher
(d) dramatic entrance of Shark
(e) the confrontation
(f) the fight

🎵 Read through the scene. Select music for the opening to suggest mood, season, time of day.

💡 How can the lighting help establish the atmosphere for the opening of this scene?

👥 Villagers – ask yourselves the following questions:
(a) Who are you?
(b) How do you earn your living?
(c) What do you think of Twilight?
(d) What do you think of the headwoman Wander?

NOVEL INTO PLAY: *The Dream Time*, Henry Treece

EIGHTH VILLAGER [*laughing*]   Beaten into shape you might say!
   [*General laughter.*]

NINTH VILLAGER   They say he was looking for someone when he came to us ... someone from the Foxfolk by the name of Blackbird. The headwoman does not like to hear of this other one who wears his carving round her neck.
   [*Villagers go on talking and working.*]

BOY [*running and shouting*]   Fish folk, the Fish folk are coming in their boats.

WANDER   How many boats? How many Fish folk?

BOY   Two bands of them and three men in each boat. It is a war band and the chief in the first boat is called Shark.

TWILIGHT   Did you see closely this chief called Shark?

BOY   Yes, he has red hair and blue eyes and carries an axe of whalebone.

TWILIGHT   He is the fiercest of men.

WANDER   It will not be easy for our war-men to drive them away. What shall we do Twilight?

TWILIGHT   Who am I to tell war-men what to do, I cannot fight.

ADDER [*running, kneeling to Twilight*]   What shall we do master? There are two of them to

> ⸺ Who are you? Where have you been? Are you excited? Afraid?
> ⸺ You are the headwoman. What have you discovered about yourself from reading this scene?

> ⸺ Why not?

one of us. What shall we do? You must tell us.

VILLAGERS   Tell us master what to do.

FIRST VILLAGER   We must fight, that's what we must do.

SECOND VILLAGER   Our war-men must protect their women and children.

THIRD VILLAGER   We have our spears to answer theirs.
[*The war-men collect their spears and encircle the women and children.*]

> 📖 How will you build up and relax the tension during this scene?

TWILIGHT   If you fight they will kill us all and take the women and children away with them. If we run away they will take the village and the River Folk will never have a place to be in again.

VILLAGERS TOGETHER   Then tell us, what can we do? Use your magic. Show your power.

TWILIGHT [*hesitates*]   If I had to decide, I would say that we should talk to them and ask them to go back to their own place and leave us alone.
[*General amazement, some polite laughter, much fear.*]

> 💬 What do these comments tell you about the villagers themselves and their attitude towards the situation they are faced with?

> 💬 Why do you hesitate? What are you thinking and feeling at this moment?

WANDER [*sternly*]   If you say this, we will do this. But they will not listen to us.

BOY WATCHER   Here they come ... they have left their boats and wave their axes.
[*Shark and his party of war-men*

> 📖 How can you work with music and lighting to highlight the dramatic effect of Shark's entrance?

NOVEL INTO PLAY: *The Dream Time*, Henry Treece

> enter. Shark's face is covered in white clay. His body is marked with x-ray paintings of fish. His men are also marked but less vividly. Shark, grinning, steps up to face Twilight. Silence.]
>
> *How do the war-men enter?*
> *Consider arranging a sequence of movement which displays their war-like qualities.*

Reading and talking

Read aloud, in groups, both the prose and play extracts.
- How closely does the play text follow that of the novel?
- Which dialogue is left exactly as it is written in the novel?
- What changes have been made to the dialogue? Why do you think they were necessary?
- Why do you think nine villagers were introduced into the playscript, but not named?
- What has been cut out from the playscript that was included in the novel? Can you think of reasons?

Drama reading and talking

- Working in groups, prepare an effective reading of the extract from the playscript. Some time spent discussing the character questions should help you to give a more thoughtful and interesting final play reading.
- Talk about the producer's role in presenting this extract for sharing with an audience. She will have to make decisions, together with those responsible, for:
  – the setting;
  – music and sound effects;
  – lighting,
  as well as directing the movements of the actors.
- How far do you think the 'messages in the margin' help with the overall production? Are there any other questions you would have included?

Talking and writing

- In pairs, re-read the whole of the *prose* extract.
- Write your own drama script to follow on from the entrance of Shark to Twilight's words: 'I shall never take up a spear again'.
  Keep to the same script layout, leaving a wide margin on the right to add your 'messages' when you have

Experimenting with form

completed the final draft of the script.
- Share your work. Unless you reproduce copies of your script, you will have to make the best of a two-person reading. Be prepared to talk about your adaptation and to make any changes you think necessary after the reading and discussion.
- After a whole class discussion, choose one or two of the most effective scripts for typing.

Drawing This is the illustration which was designed for the cover of the whole playscript.

Drama   Design a suitable and exciting cover to illustrate the particular scene you have been working on.

You might decide to present the whole scene as:
- a polished play reading;
- a prepared drama performance; or
- part of a programme in which you introduce the whole book to another group – your own art and written work could be included in such a presentation.

VERSE PLAYS

The Gift of a Lamb, Charles Causley

Great stories such as are found in the Bible and in the myths and legends of many lands have often inspired the writing of verse plays. It is not surprising that the poet Charles Causley, who has written many ballads, should have chosen to write a verse play based on the story of Christmas.

We take up the story at the point at which the three shepherds are introduced.

[*Lights come up to reveal the summit of a gently-sloping hill. It is winter. On the R. slope are three shepherds:* BEN, *a grizzled grandfather,* JOHN *his son, and* DAN *his grandson, all well-wrapped against the cold. By them are sticks or staves, a pack of food, and one or two leather bottles. They also have, respectively, a fiddle, pipe and a drum at hand.* JOHN's *whistle-pipe is tucked in his belt. A fire glows. The dim outlines of sheep may be seen.* BEN, *leaning on a shepherd's crook, stands at the lowest level.* DAN *is seated by the fire, on which a pot of broth is being heated.* JOHN, *nearest the top of the hill, peers into the darkness watchfully.*
Music for song.]

STORYTELLER   But as they played
So sweet and clear,
A stranger crept
Their pasture near;
And even as

Experimenting with form

> The shepherds played,
> A stranger crept
> From shade to shade.
> He did not stand
> Beneath the sky
> And greet the shepherds
> Eye to eye;
> He did not sing,
> He did not hum –
> He wished no man
> To hear him come,
> But secretly
> And without sound
> He crawled across
> The glimmering ground;
> Over the meadow,
> Up the hill,
> To where the sheep and lambs
> Lay still.
> His brow and neck
> He'd smudged with soot,
> And on his face
> A mask he'd put.
> He carried on his back
> A sack,
> And the name of the man
> Was
> Thieving Jack.

[*Lights come up on the L. slope of the hill. What at first seems to be a rock or boulder slowly begins to move. It is* THIEVING JACK. *The shepherds' music is heard a little distance off, and held behind his voice as he begins to speak.*]

THIEVING JACK   Hark to the silly shepherds
    As they sing and as they play –
    Though what they've got to sing about
    Is more than I can say.
    A shepherd's lot is 'eavy,
    An' a shepherd's lot is poor
    In every kind o' weather you can think of –
    An' some more!
    They works by night an' day –

VERSE PLAYS: *The Gift of a Lamb*, Charles Causley

Why, it's enough to make yer weep!
If you ask me, a shepherd's
Just as silly as 'is sheep.
But that's 'is silly business,
An' as for mine, my friends,
You won't catch *me* a-workin'
All the hours the good Lord sends.
I likes to eat, I likes to drink,
I likes to lie-a-bed;
I calls no man *my* master –
'Ere's what I do instead:
I nicks a little chicken
Or I bags a side o' beef,
So guard yer goods when I'm about
Because I am

        a

          thief!

I robs the rich AND poor –
You never
Met a worse than me:
For anything that's *yours*
Is mine,
And mine's me own,
You see.
No ducks that quack
Are safe from Jack,
Nor any sow that squealed;
Nor any sheep or lamb that's left
Unguarded in the field.
And O, but it's a lamb this night
On which I've got me eye –
I liked the black and white of it
As I went passing by.
An' so among the rocks I creep,
An' Opens up me sack . . .
[*Very faint bleat of a lamb.*]
An' slips the lambkin in –
[*Slightly louder bleat.*]
NOW!
It belongs to Thieving Jack!

225

[*Bleat.* THIEVING JACK *chuckles. Bell begins to sound midnight. Light fades L. and increases R.* SHEPHERDS *play and sing on the hill.*]

BEN   [*sings*] Now the bell at midnight
           Chimes to make us glad,
           Bringing in the birthday
           Of a shepherd lad.

JOHN   [*sings*] He shall have a wooden crook,
           A smock as clean as light;
           He shall have a lambkin
           Whose wool is black and white.

[*Bell ceases striking. Light begins to grow in the sky above the* SHEPHERDS. *The echo of the bell's last note becomes a sustained, metallic sound held behind the following:*]

DAN   [*alarmed*] Good father, and grandfather dear,
           What is that light, I pray,
           That burns above us in the sky
           And turns the night to day?
           Each spike of grass, each stone, is bright
           Upon the midnight hill –
           Yet lamb and sheep they soundly sleep,
           And silent are, and still.

JOHN   [*gazing up, wondering*] Such fire it comes not from the stars,
           Nor comes it from the moon –
           And bolder is it than the sun
           That blazes at the noon.

BEN   My children, kneel;
           My children, pray
           That God may give us grace,
           For none may know when he must go
           To meet him face to face:
           [*Music*]
           Here is a holy place.

[*Music. More light. Three* ANGELS *appear in the sky above the summit of the hill. Music behind the following:*]

1ST ANGEL   Fear not, shepherds, for I bring
                Tidings of a new-born King –

VERSE PLAYS: *The Gift of a Lamb*, Charles Causley

	Not in castle, not in keep, Nor in tower tall and steep; Not in manor-house or hall, But a humble ox's stall.
2ND ANGEL	Underneath a standing star And where sheep and cattle are, In a bed of straw and hay God's own Son is born this day. If to Bethlehem you go, This the truth you soon shall know.
3RD ANGEL	And as signal and as sign, Sure as all the stars that shine, You shall find him, shepherds all, Swaddled in a baby-shawl; And the joyful news will share With good people everywhere.
2ND ANGEL	Therefore, listen as we cry:
THREE ANGELS	Glory be to God on high, And his gifts of love and peace To his people never cease.

[*Light and music fade on* ANGELS. *A moment of silence. The* SHEPHERDS, *bewildered, exchange glances, shake their heads, rub their eyes.*]

DAN	Grandfather, O tell me clear, Did *you* see and did *you* hear Angel-voices, angel-gleam? Do I wake? Or do I dream?
BEN	[*reassuring*] Why, indeed the angels came ...
JOHN	[*quickly*] And I heard and saw the same ...
BEN	So, with swift and fearful tread, Let us to that cattle-shed.
DAN	But the night is dark and deep. Who will watch the lambs and sheep?
BEN	Dearest grandson, do not fear; God will keep them safely here: Guard the hill and guard the plain

Experimenting with form

> Soundly till we come again.
> [*He smiles, and removes the pot from the fire.*]

JOHN   Then let's music play . . .

DAN   And sing!

BEN   For we go to greet a King!
[*Music.*]

SHEPHERDS   [*sing*] High in the heaven
A gold star burns
Lighting our way
As the great world turns.

Silver the frost
It shines on the stem
As we now journey
To Bethlehem.

White is the ice
At our feet as we tread,
Pointing a path
To the manger-bed.

Reading

Working in small groups, prepare this extract for presentation. As you rehearse your parts, you might find the following points helpful:

- It is not easy to read rhymed verse which has a regular rhythm – avoid 'sing-song', go for the meaning!
- Experiment with the part of the storyteller as a piece of choral speaking, if the whole group or class is to be involved.
- Think about how to bring out differences of age and attitudes in the three shepherds. Accents might help.
- Thieving Jack has a long speech to make. He is obviously a likeable rogue with a sense of humour. Decide how to vary the pace and use pauses, so that you hold your listener's interest and bring out the comedy and drama in the speech. What kind of accent do you think he has?
- The 'singing' parts can be spoken – you could use the storyteller, the choral speaking group or Ben and John speaking together in order to show that it is not 'normal' conversation.

- Decide how to speak the 'angel' parts which should provide a contrast to the shepherds and Thieving Jack. Choose three people with voices different from each other in tone.

PROSE INTO PLAY

The Maid Who Chose a Husband, retold by Efua Sutherland

We have chosen an unusual folk tale from Ghana in West Africa for you to read and rework as a verse play.

The maid of Kyerefaso, the Queen Mother's daughter, was as nimble as a deer and wise as an owl. Foruwa, such was she, with head held high, eyes soft and wide with wonder. And she was light of foot, light in all her movements.

As she stepped along the water path like a young deer that had strayed from the thicket, as she sprang along the water path, she was a picture to give the eye a feast. And nobody passed her by but turned to look at her again.

Those of her village said that her voice was like the murmur of a river quietly flowing beneath the shadows of bamboo leaves. They said her smile blossomed like a lily on her lips and rose like the sun.

Butterflies do not fly away from flowers; and Foruwa was the flower of the village. So all the village butterflies tried to draw near her at every turn, crossed and criss-crossed her path. Men said of her, 'She shall be my wife, and mine, and mine, and mine.'

But suns rose and set, moons waxed and waned, and as the days passed Foruwa became no man's wife. She smiled at the butterflies and waved her hand lightly to greet them as she went swiftly about her work, saying, 'Morning, Kweku. Morning, Kwesi. Morning, Kwodo.' That was all.

So they said, even while their hearts thumped for her, 'Proud! Foruwa is too proud.'

When they came together, the men would say, 'There goes a silly girl. She is not just stiff-in-the-neck proud, not

229

just breasts-stuck-out-I-am-the-only-girl-in-the-village proud. What kind of pride is that?'

The end of the year came round again, bringing the season of festivals. For the gathering-in of corn, yams and cocoa there were harvest celebrations. And there were bride-meetings too.

The Queen Mother was there, tall and wise, standing before the men, and there was silence.

'What news, what news do you bring?' she asked.

'We come with dusty brows from our path-finding, Mother. We come with weary thorn-pricked feet. We come to bathe in the coolness of your peaceful stream. We come to offer our manliness to create new life.'

'It is well. Come, maidens, women all, join the men in dance, for they offer themselves to create new life.'

Yet there was one girl who did not dance.

'What, Foruwa, will you not dance?' asked the Queen Mother.

Foruwa opened her lips and this was all she said. 'I do not find him here.'

'Who? Who do you not find, daughter?'

'He with whom I wish to create new life. He is not here, Mother. These men's faces are empty; there is nothing in them, nothing at all.'

'What will become of you, my daughter?'

'The day I find him, Mother, the day I find the man, I shall come running to let you know.'

That evening there was heard a new song in the village:

> 'There was a woman long ago,
> Tell that maid, tell that maid;
> There was a woman long ago,
> Who said she would not wed Kwesi,
> She would not marry Shaw,
> She would not, would not, would not.
> One day she hurried home,
> I've found the man, the man, the man,
> Tell that maid, tell that maid,
> Her man looked like a chief,
> Most splendid to behold.
> But he turned into a python,
> He turned into a python
> And swallowed the maid whole.'

From then on there were some in the village who turned their backs on Foruwa as she passed.

But a day came when Foruwa came running to her mother. She burst through the courtyard gate, and there she stood breathless in the yard, full of joy. And a stranger walked in after her and stood beside her, tall and strong as a pillar.

'Here he is, Mother, here is the man.'

The Queen Mother took a slow look at the stranger standing there as strong as a forest tree, and said, 'You bear the light of wisdom on your face, my son. You are welcome. But tell me who you are?'

'Greetings, Mother,' said the stranger. 'I am a worker. My hands are all I have to offer, for they are all my wealth. I have journeyed to see how folk work in other lands. I have that knowledge and my strength. Together, Foruwa and I will build our lives. That is my story.'

Strange as the story is, the stranger was given in marriage to Foruwa.

Soon, quite soon, the people of Kyerefaso began to take notice of Foruwa and the stranger in quite a different way.

'See them work together,' some said. 'They who mingle sweat and song, they for whom toil is joy and life is full and abundant.'

'See,' said others, 'what a harvest the land yields under their care.'

'They have taken the earth and moulded it into bricks. See what a home they have built and how it graces the village.'

'Look at the craft of their fingers – the baskets and kente cloth, the stools and mats – together they make them all.'

'And our children crowd about them, gazing at them with wonder and delight.'

Then it did not satisfy them any more to sit all day at their games beneath the mango trees.

'See what Foruwa and her husband have done together,' they declared. 'Shall the daughters and sons of the land not do the same?'

And soon they too were toiling and their fields began to yield as never before. A new spirit stirred the village. The unkempt houses disappeared one by one and new homes were built after Foruwa's and the stranger's appeared. It

231

seemed as if the village of Kyerefaso had been born anew.

The people themselves became more alive and a new pride possessed them. They were no longer just grabbing from the land what they desired for their comfort and for their stomach's hunger. They were looking at the land with new eyes, feeling it in their blood, and building a beautiful place for themselves and their children. And they did it all, women and men, together.

'Osee!' sang the villagers.

It was festival time again.

'Osee! we are the creators. We shall build a new life with our strength. We shall create it with our minds.'

Following the men and the women came the children. On their heads they carried every kind of produce that the land had yielded and the crafts their fingers had made. Green plantains and yellow bananas were carried by the bunch in large white wooden trays. Garden eggs, tomatoes, red oil-palm nuts warmed by the sun were piled high in black earthen vessels. Oranges, yams and maize filled shining brass trays and golden calabashes. Girls and boys were proudly carrying coloured mats and baskets, and toys that they had made themselves.

The Queen Mother watched the procession gathering on the village square, now emerald green from recent rains. She watched the people moving in a happy dance towards her as she stood outside her house.

She saw Foruwa. Her pile of charcoal in a large brass tray, adorned with red hibiscus, danced and swayed with her body. Happiness filled the Queen Mother when she saw her daughter thus.

Then she saw Foruwa's husband. He was carrying a white lamb in his arms, and he was singing happily with the other men and women. The Queen Mother looked on him with pride.

The procession now approached the royal house.

'See how she stands waiting, our Queen Mother. Spread the skins of gentle sheep before her, gently, gently. Spread the yield of the land before her. Spread the craft of your hands before her, gently, gently. Spread the fruit of men's and women's work together at her feet.

'For she is life.'

PROSE INTO PLAY: *The Maid Who Chose a Husband*, Efua Sutherland

Reading and notemaking

- Read through the story. Make a list of the characters who are named.
- Before you write your first draft of the verse play, think about:
  - the use of a storyteller (narrator) and a chorus, e.g. villagers, suitors;
  - any lines or verses which you might use straight from the story;
  - the sequence of events – what to include and what to leave out;
  - using a mixture of free and rhymed verse forms;
  - the need for using language appropriate to the telling of the story.

We asked a group of second-year pupils to rewrite the folk tale as a verse play. This is how they began:

The Maid of Kyerefaso
A tale from Ghana in West Africa

Characters   Maid: Foruwa
Queen Mother
Villagers: Kwodo, Kwesi, Shaw, Kweku
Husband/Stranger
Storyteller

STORYTELLER   There was a woman long ago
Tell that maid, tell that maid;
There was a woman long ago,
Who said she would not wed Kwesi,
She would not marry Shaw.
She would not, would not, would not.

VILLAGERS   One day she hurried home,
'I've found the man, the man, the man.'
Tell that maid, tell that maid;
Her man looked like a chief,
Most splendid to behold.
But he turned into a python,
He turned into a python
And swallowed the maid whole.

FORUWA   My name is Foruwa
And, so they say,

233

Experimenting with form

>   I'm as wise as an owl
>   And as bright as the day.
>   When villagers see me
>   They take another glance,
>   For I'm as graceful as a swan
>   Or a butterfly in dance.
>
> VILLAGERS We villagers adore her;
>   It is she we wish to wed,
>   But Foruwa is too proud
>   Or so her suitors said
>
> KWODO   For she does not want to marry me
>
> KWESI   Nor me
>
> SHAW   Nor me
>
> KWEKU   Nor me!

Discussion and writing

- What decisions do you think they must have made before writing their first draft?
- Now, write your own verse play using their version as your starting point.

7 Fact, feeling and form

ANTHOLOGY
Tell Me About the Rabbits

An anthology can be a collection of every kind of writing; it may include fact as well as fiction and illustrations; prose, poems or plays.

You may be asked to produce your own anthology, either based on a particular theme or with complete freedom to choose any subject. The first factor you must bear in mind is the audience for whom your work is intended.

Here is an example of an anthology which we called 'Tell Me About the Rabbits' (a quotation from *Of Mice And Men* by John Steinbeck). The following extracts are taken from two parts of the anthology, 'Rabbits in the Wild' and 'Rabbits as Pets'.

The Private Life of the Rabbit, Lockley

Death from shock is known in many animals, from man to bird. We have taken up small wild birds, caught in outhouses or ringing traps, which have been in a coma of fright, prostrate, heart beating violently but otherwise unhurt, and some have never recovered; while others actually appear to feign death or coma, and will suddenly fly away, fully alert. The latter behaviour is akin to that of the rabbit and hare, which will often crouch perfectly still, as if in a trance, in order to escape the notice of a passerby; we have sometimes been able to pounce on and hold a crouching rabbit or hare.

Rabbits pursued by stoat or weasel, muskrats pursued by mink, caribou by wolf, have been recorded as slowing down

235

Fact, feeling and form

in their escape flight, then dragging their legs helplessly or standing still and showing symptoms of paralysis, which enables the pursuer to close upon the pursued almost at leisure.

Rabbits are so human. Or is it the other way round – humans are so rabbit?

All Things Come of Age, Liam O'Flaherty

And then, as he lay crouching, he began to feel afraid. It was the same feeling he experienced a few days previously, when his last remaining brother, having hopped into the clump of briars on the left, had suddenly begun to scream. There was a strange feeling in the air, the nearness of a sinister force, that prevented movement. At that time, however, he had been able to move after a little while and run into his burrow. Now it was different.

The sinister feeling increased. There was absolute silence and there was nothing strange to smell and yet he felt the approach of the sinister force, something unknown and monstrous. In spite of himself, although he wanted awfully to hide from it, he looked in the direction whence he sensed the approach of the enemy. His head shook violently as he glanced towards the boulders that lay across the stream. And then he began to scream. A weasel was crossing the line of boulders.

The baby rabbit had never before seen a weasel, but the long brown body, that moved with awful speed, making no sound, drove him crazy with horror. The weasel paused in the middle of the stream, raised his powerful head and stared at the rabbit, his wicked eyes fixed. And then, keeping his head raised and his eyes on his prey, he glided like a flash to the bank. He disappeared for a fraction of a second behind a stone in his path and then appeared again, standing against the little stone, staring fixedly. Now his powerful head, raised above the long brown barrel of his body, was like the boss of a hammer, poised to strike. The rabbit's screaming became wilder. He was now completely in the brute's power, mesmerized by the staring eyes and by the sinister presence.

Fact, feeling and form

9

'He ... appeared ... standing against the little stone, staring fixedly.'

Bye Baby Bunting

'Bye baby bunting,
Daddy's gone a-hunting,
Gone to get a rabbit skin
To wrap the baby bunting in.'

Here I Am with My Rabbits

Buy a Rabbet a Rabbet

Here I am with my rabbits
Hanging on my pole,
The finest Hampshire rabbits
That e'er crept from a hole.

Fifteen Rabbits, Felix Salten

Hops had grown to be a lusty fellow and, whenever an opportunity offered, loved nothing better than boldly and greedily to stuff himself to the full. Often he was so plunged in gluttony that for whole moments he would neglect that prime rule of every rabbit's existence – timid cautiousness.

Suddenly he noticed that all his comrades had scattered.

It flashed through his mind that he had heard the danger signals of the jay and squirrel. Now, though they were silent, he seemed to hear them, and went numb with fear.

*

Above him, in the old beech, a squirrel ran along a stout branch, sat on the extreme tip that swayed gently, held both his forepaws pleadingly in front of his glossy, white breast and screamed down at him, 'Almighty tree-trunk! Are you still there!'

He instantly whisked around again and scampered into the thick foliage high up in the top of the tree, so that all you could see of his bushy tail was a thin, red streak, twitching among the leaves.

Hops remained motionless.

His heart began to beat wildly.

He breathed in the wind so deeply that his whiskers twitched violently. Nothing! The wind brought him no scent.

Hops raised his ears.

Then, opposite him in the tall woods, where a light wind was stirring, he heard a very soft crackling in the trampled, tender underbrush, heard a very gentle pattering and rustle of footsteps. Two-legged!

Hops sat up on his hind legs. He sat up straight as an arrow, his long ears erect, his whiskers, his handsome whiskers, aquiver, his clear, round eyes so wide open in their anxiety that you could see their whites.

Then, between the tree-trunks in the tall woods, he beheld the gigantic, mysterious being who walks erect on two legs, Him whom every creature in the forest fears more than any other.

Harvest Rabbit, a recipe

Allow 1 small rabbit to every two persons.
Dripping.
3 prunes to each rabbit.
A bunch of fresh herbs to each rabbit.
Seasoned flour.
Onions (large, or salad onions).
1 thin slice of fat bacon to each rabbit.
Stock.

Forcemeat balls:
Chopped bacon (or suet).
Chives (or young onion tops).
Sweet marjoram.
Parsley.
Seasoning.
Breadcrumbs.
1 or 2 eggs.

Skin, draw and cut off the heads, scuts and feet of the rabbits. Wash well, leave in salt water for 15 minutes, then dry and fry whole in dripping until a pale golden brown all over. Drain, and stuff under the ribs of each 3 well-soaked prunes and a bunch of fresh herbs. Coat thickly with well-seasoned flour. Cover the bottom of a large deep baking-dish with thinly sliced onions, or the bulbs of salad onions, lay the floured rabbits on them, with a thin slice of fat bacon over each, and just cover with stock. Bake slowly for 2 hours.

Serve on a hot dish, garnished with the onions and plenty of large forcemeat balls, made of the ingredients above bound with the egg, or 2 eggs if as many as 3 rabbits are cooked.

Fry a deep brown, and be sure that plenty of fresh herb is used, as they must cut a bright green. Strain the gravy, and serve separately.

From Mrs Jennifer Dane, Buckinghamshire.

Peter Rabbit, Beatrix Potter

'NOW, my dears,' said old Mrs. Rabbit one morning, ' you may go into the fields or down the lane, but don't go into Mr. McGregor's garden: your Father had an accident there; he was put in a pie by Mrs. McGregor.'

The Private Life of the Rabbit, Lockley

In the autumn of 1953 the disease of myxomatosis appeared in rabbits in south-east England. It spread within a year over most of the British Isles, mowing down rabbit populations spectacularly. Farmers and foresters, whose crops and trees had suffered from over-population of rabbits, were suddenly relieved of an expensive pest, and were financially better off as a result of myxomatosis. But the appearance of the affected rabbits, with swollen heads, blind and deaf, and wandering helplessly along roads and fields, aroused a national indignation and outcry. 'Mercy squads' of men and women, chiefly from the towns, were set up by the Royal Society for the Prevention of Cruelty to Animals and other humanitarian organisations, to go forth and shoot or cudgel these dying rabbits to a more speedy death.

Myxomatosis, Philip Larkin

Caught in the centre of a soundless field
While hot inexplicable hours go by
'What trap is this? Where were its teeth concealed?'
You seem to ask.
              I make a sharp reply,
Then clean my stick. I'm glad I can't explain
Just in what jaws you were to suppurate.
You may have thought things would come right again
If you could only keep quite still and wait.

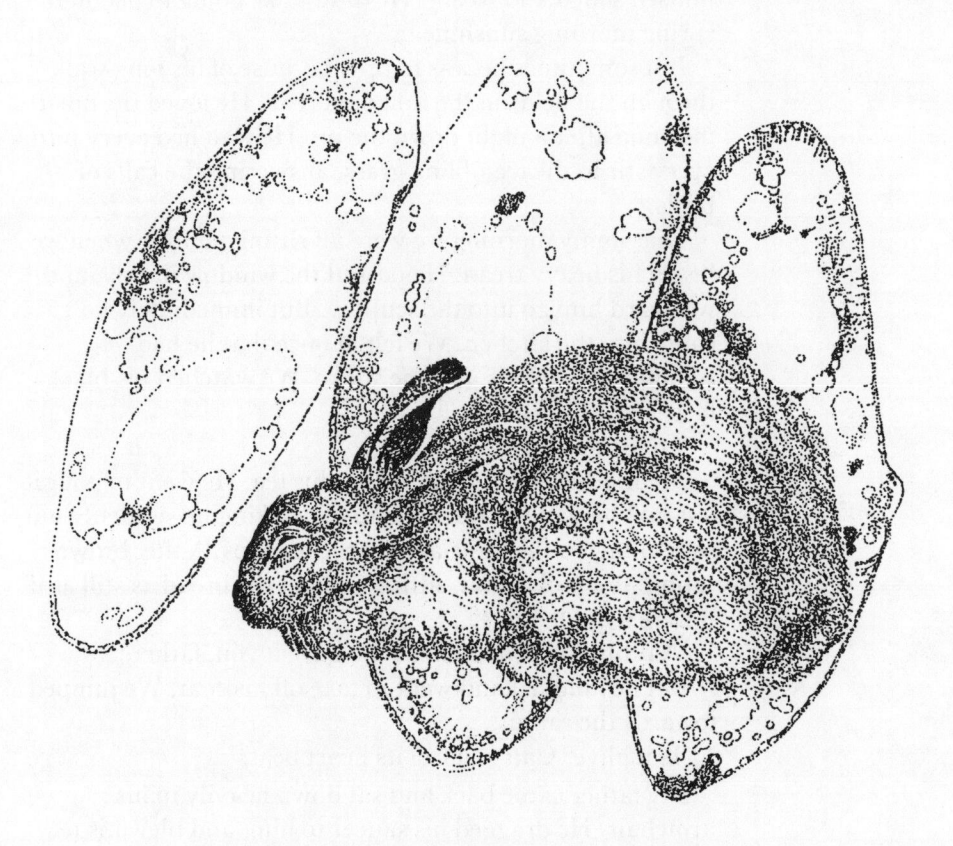

It is estimated that the increase of agricultural production since the success of myxomatosis in the south-eastern States of Australia has been worth some £50,000,000 annually.

Rabbits as pets

Adolf, D.H. Lawrence

When we were children our father often worked at night. Once it was springtime, and he used to arrive home, black and tired, just as we were downstairs in our nightdresses. Then night met morning face to face, and the meeting was not always happy. Perhaps it was painful to my father to see us gaily entering upon the day into which he dragged himself soiled and weary. He didn't like going to bed in the spring morning sunshine.

But sometimes he was happy, because of his long walk through the fields in the first daybreak. He loved the open morning after a night down the pit. He watched every bird, every stir in the trembling grass, answering the calls of birds.

One sunny morning we were all sitting at table when we heard his heavy tread. He passed the window darkly, and we heard him go into the scullery. But immediately he came into the kitchen. We felt at once that he had something to tell us. No one spoke. We watched his black face for a second.

'Give me a drink', he said.

My mother hastily poured out his tea. He went to pour it out into his saucer. But instead of drinking he suddenly put something on the table among the teacups. A tiny brown rabbit! A small rabbit, sitting against the bread as still as if it were a made thing.

'A rabbit! A young one! Who gave it you, father?'

But he laughed and went to take off his coat. We jumped towards the rabbit.

'Is it alive? Can you feel its heart beat?'

My father came back and sat down heavily in his armchair. He dragged his saucer to him, and blew his tea, pushing out his red lips under his black moustache.

'Where did you get it, father?'

'I picked it up,' he said, wiping his naked forearm over his mouth and beard.

'Where?'

'It is a wild one!' came my mother's quick voice.

'Yes, it is.'

'Then why did you bring it?' cried my mother.

'Oh, we wanted it,' came our cry.

'Yes, I've no doubt you did . . .' answered my mother sharply. But she was drowned in the noise of our questions.

On the field path my father had found a dead mother rabbit and three dead little ones – this one alive, but unmoving.

'But what killed them, father?'

'I couldn't say, my child. I should think she had eaten something.'

'Why did you bring it?' again my mother's voice of blame. 'You know what it will be.'

My father made no answer, but we were loud in disagreement.

When morning came and it was light, I went downstairs. Opening the scullery door, I heard a slight movement. Then I saw drops of milk all over the floor. And there was the rabbit, the tops of his ears showing behind a pair of boots. He sat bright-eyed, moving his nose and looking at me while not looking at me.

He was alive – very much alive.

'Father!' My father stopped at the door. 'Father, the rabbit's alive.'

'Of course,' he said.

'Mind how you go in.'

By evening, however, the little creature was tame, quite tame.

It's the boot for 'Flopears'

HARD TIMES MEAN SCHOOL RABBITS HAVE GOT TO GO

by PAUL JOHN

IT was heartbreak for 450 children at Shears Green Junior School, Northfleet, this week when they were told that their 26 pet rabbits are to be victims of the economy axe.

One teacher said the children were 'dismayed and subdued' by the news.

'It was mainly because the children who are staying have been looking forward to being involved in our animal centre and looking after the animals. Now all they feel is disappointment,' he said.

'One or two were in tears when we told them,' he added.

The rabbits must go because the teacher in charge of them has left and the County Council's 'freeze' on staff recruitment means he cannot be replaced.

With more than 40 other assorted animals and birds in the school's animal centre and a general 'tightening of the belt', Headmaster Mr John Hales no longer has time to take care of the rabbits.

He told me: 'I can cope with the guinea pigs, the doves and the tortoises. But I cannot cope with a multiplicity of rabbits.'

It seems that Mr Hales' problem is growing all the time with a small 'boom' in the school's rabbit population by 23 this term. He has already given away 10 to local rabbit lovers.

News of the Shears Green rabbit problem came at a time when the local branch of the National Confederation of Parent-Teacher Associations was warning parents about the serious position education is now in.

Mr Hales, a spokesman for the branch said: 'It is a fact that the Government was given a clear mandate to keep expenditure in the public sector as low as possible.

'It is also a fact that many local education authorities have been elected on a declared programme to reduce wasteful spending to a minimum.

'However, there is a point beyond which reduction of expenditure must damage the quality of education to an unacceptable degree,' he added.

It is now just over a month since Kent County Council's Policy and Resources Committee announced that it would pursue a 'vigorous' policy of restraint of staff recruitment in all departments for an initial period of one month.

But, there are signs that this initial period will be extended—probably until well into the autumn.

In present climate

Amongst the county's primary schools the 'freeze' means that the 'county formula' of teacher/pupil ratios cannot be exceeded and that no extra staff can be recruited nor replaced should they leave. Inevitably, this means a cut in some services.

Mr Hales said he recognises that the education authorities are unable to prevent this situation but he wants parents to know that, in the present climate 'some things have got to go.'

'What have got to go in our case are the rabbits,' he said.

ANTHOLOGY: 'It's the Boot for Flopears'

Two boys with pet rabbits: detail from a modern window in St Luke's Church, Stickney, Lincolnshire. The window is inscribed: 'In memory of those children who have no other memorial.'

Fact, feeling and form

Reading

'Anthology reading' invites you to dip in, to browse and to linger. Choose your own way of 'reading' and talking about 'Tell Me About the Rabbits'.

Talking and writing

- Choose one of the pieces of material (either writing or an illustration) and jot down notes which will help you to introduce it as part of a group or class discussion on 'Rabbits in the Wild' or 'Rabbits as Pets'.
- Share one of your experiences which you have been reminded of by any of the pieces in the anthology.
- Focus on the material on pages 235–8 in which we learn about what happens when rabbits are pursued by weasels.
  – What evidence is there in the story to show that Liam O'Flaherty has closely observed the behaviour of rabbits in this situation?
  – How does the story deepen your understanding of the *facts*?
  – Does the factual information help you to appreciate the story?
  – Is there anything to show that Lockley is writing from a personal viewpoint?
  – Make a list of the verbs which Liam O'Flaherty uses in his last paragraph. Use some of his, and add appropriate ones of your own, to write a short poem in which you describe the meeting between the rabbit and the weasel. Give your poem an interesting title.
- Read the factual information, the poem and look at the illustration on pages 242–3 (myxomatosis).
  – What words and lines in the poem show the effects of the disease on the rabbit?
  – What is the effect of having the rabbit 'seem to ask' the words in inverted commas?

Can we ever say that stories and poems are all fiction, and non-fiction all fact?

Writers of stories and poems must know some facts about their chosen subject and skilled writers of non-fiction are concerned with feeling and the form in which they present their information.

– Does a re-reading of Lockley's description of the spread

ANTHOLOGY: 'It's the Boot for Flopears'

and effects of myxomatosis convince you that he, like the poet, is also making a *personal* comment?
– Which key words point to his attitude towards this method of pest control?

Aneurin Edwards makes a non-verbal comment in his drawing of an infected rabbit against a background of diseased blood cells.

– Discuss the impact of the illustration on your thinking and feeling about myxomatosis.
– If the artist had chosen to illustrate the whole *poem* instead of the *title* word, what would he have had to include in his drawing?

Very few attempts to care for young wild, and sometimes injured, creatures ever succeed. We are urged to leave lost young birds where they have fallen in the hope that they might be looked after by the parent bird until they recover strength and fly again.

Reading, talking and writing

Re-read all the material in this section and the Penelope Lively extract in 'Finding A Focus', pages 65–6.
- Describe an incident in which you find a damaged creature. You could include:
  – details of the place;
  – the condition of the creature;
  – reactions from other people (shown through thoughtful use of conversation as used by D. H. Lawrence in *Adolf*);
  – the outcome of your efforts.
  As well as being *accurate* in your description, you will need to find a way of sharing your thoughts and feelings.
- What kind of contact with animals or insects did you have in your primary school?
  – What are the advantages of keeping classroom pets?
  – Are there any disadvantages?
  – When pets are in classrooms occupied by young children, what rules and regulations should be observed?
  – Write a notice or draw a poster, for use in a primary school classroom, setting out your rules.

- Write letters from children and adults in response to the newspaper article. Try to express a variety of points of view including facts as well as feelings.
- What particular characteristics of the rabbit make it an appealing pet?
- Write a poem or piece of descriptive writing based on an occasion when someone (it could be you) is forced to part with a domestic animal which s/he has had for a long time.
- Talk about the memorial window to children in St Luke's Church, Stickney (on page 247).

Fact, feeling and form

One of the ways through which you, as a reader, can collect, select and arrange material to present a variety of points of view and make a personal comment, is to compile your own anthology.

As a compiler, you will need to write an introduction and make connecting links between one part and another. You are also given the opportunity to include some of your own work.

Some guidelines
- Keep the subject matter strictly under control. Think small – it's *trains* not *transport*!
- Collect a variety of material and then limit your selection to a number of pieces, say ten, including illustrations.
- For your *bibliography*, make a note of the title, author/artist, publisher and date of publication.
- Arrange your material so that even in the placing of one piece alongside another you are making an observation, e.g. Mrs Rabbit's warning to the children follows a recipe for Harvest Rabbit.
- You will probably find it easier to write a short introduction to your anthology when you have finished organising the material.
- Be prepared to rewrite some of the 'factual' material so that it has your 'voice' in it. There is no real satisfaction in copying out chunks of information which you don't understand.

- Take care to present your work so that you are pleased with the way it looks. Other pupils in the class might be asked to illustrate one of your own pieces of writing or the cover. Consider also the use of greetings cards, wrapping paper and photographs.
- Use a word processor to help you to decide the layout of each page.
- A 'jumbo' typewriter might be used to create a different type-face and so add interest.
- Any lettering or headings should be carefully checked for accuracy, especially if some words or names are unfamiliar.
- Finally, avoid the temptation to choose a subject which has been over-anthologised; think of our original idea 'Tell me about . . .' and jot down what interests you or what you would like to know more about. If you decide to add to this topic then here is a list of possible areas to start you looking for more poems, stories, reference material and illustrations:
  - Rabbit legends and superstitions.
  - Rabbit jokes, limericks and fun poems.
  - Rabbits in literature – from picture books to novels.
  - The life history of the rabbit.